NEW YORK STATE TROOPER EXAM GUIDE

Angelo Tropea

ISBN-13: 978-1545548776
ISBN-10: 1545548773

Published by Angelo Tropea

The passages, examples and questions used in this book are for study purposes only and do not reflect official names, codes, policies, rules or procedures of any governmental or public or private business, agency or department.

Unless otherwise clearly indicated, any similarity of names of persons, addresses, places and telephone numbers used in this book to any actual names of persons, addresses and telephone numbers is purely coincidental.

The information and web addresses presented in this book are current as of publication date. Always consult the official governmental web sites and other relevant web sites for the most up-to-date information.

CONTENTS

1. TEST-TAKING SUGGESTIONS

1. Rest the day before the exam. The night before the exam is not a good time to go to a party or to a sports game. Scientific studies have shown that sleep deprivation dulls the mind.

2. If at all possible, try not to cram. If you wish, just REVIEW the exercises, suggestions and hints, and practice test. If you have been studying correctly, you owe it to yourself to rest. Cramming the day before the exam often hurts instead of helping. Pace yourself each day and you will reduce your chances of getting test anxiety.

3. Pay careful attention to the time and location of the test site. Plan to get there in comfort and without having to rush. For more than thirty years I have heard many horror stories of candidates not arriving at the test site on time.

4. Do <u>not</u> go into the test hungry. Eat and drink enough to last you through the test.

5. At the test site, listen carefully and don't take anything for granted. Follow directions carefully. Make sure that you don't miss any information that might help you get a higher score.

6. If you have time, familiarize yourself with the computer (or answer sheet) you will be using. Check to see if the computer is working properly. Examine the answer sheet and understand how they want you to mark the answers. If there are any problems, bring them to the attention of the test monitor as soon as possible.

7. Crystallize in your mind how many questions you must answer - and the types of questions.

8. Quickly develop a time budget - and during the exam check the time <u>on your watch</u> to make sure you are not falling behind. Do not rely on the monitor to keep you informed of the time.

9. Usually every question is worth the same as the other questions. Don't spend too much time on any one question (unless you have finished all the other questions and are satisfied with your answers).

10. If you find during the test that there are questions for which you believe there is more than one valid answer, do not lose time thinking about it. Select the best answer that you can - and go on.

11. Finally, if you finish early, do <u>not</u> get up and go home. If allowed, review the exam and your answers.

<u>GOOD LUCK !!!</u>

2. HOW TO PREPARE FOR THE EXAM

1. If available, read the New York State Trooper Exam Announcement. The exam announcement details the job requirements and provides insights into the exam content and screening procedures. Take advantage of any "Exam Tutorials" that may be provided.

2. Briefly "skim" the contents of this book by reading the table of contents and then looking at each section to see how the types of questions in the book correspond to the New York State Trooper Exam announcement, and any tutorials that may be provided.

3. To get the greatest benefit, try to study every day for at least half an hour – and longer (1-2 hours) if you can. Try not to have very long sessions. Studies have indicated that frequent, shorter sessions are more effective than fewer, longer ones.

4. Study in a quiet, well-lit area with as few distractions as possible. This will help you to focus and obtain the maximum benefit from each session.

5. Review sections 3 – 8 in this book. They will introduce you to the types of questions and provide practice questions with the answers explained.
Do not continue to the practice exam until you have mastered all the different types of questions. Read all the comments after each answer to reinforce important facts and test-answering techniques. Try to record your answers on a separate sheet of paper and not in the book. This will make it easier for you to return to the questions and answer them again without being influenced by your prior work.

6. Now tackle the multiple-choice Practice Exam. Pay careful attention to every question that you don't answer correctly. If necessary, review the section in the book that relates to that type of question. Try to take the practice exam in a single session (2 - 2½ hours). By doing so, you will gain a valuable understanding of how long your attention span must last during the actual exam.

7. If the test is administered on computer, make sure that <u>before</u> the test date you're familiar with the computer keyboard and the fundamentals of computer operation. If you must record your answers on a paper answer sheet, make sure that you understand how to mark the answer sheet.
At the test site, listen carefully to the directions on how to use the computer or how to mark the answer sheet, including how to change answers. If you're not certain about anything, ask questions.

8. If some questions are hard for you, keep in mind what Thomas Edison once said: "Genius is one percent inspiration and ninety-nine percent perspiration."

---

3. TYPES OF QUESTIONS

WRITTEN COMPREHENSION

These questions evaluate your ability to understand written language.

1. One version of this type of question is understanding a written passage that is provided, such as a narrative of the events of a crime, a section of law, or a written complaint.

2. Another version of this type of question may test your ability to follow written instructions that are provided.

WRITTEN EXPRESSION

These questions evaluate your ability to communicate clearly and concisely with proper words in a grammatically correct way.

1. One version of this type of question asks you to select the best way to communicate some thoughts or ideas to other persons.

2. Another version of this type of question asks you to put in a logical order four or five sentences in a sequence so that others will understand what is being communicated.

PROBLEM SENSITIVITY QUESTIONS

These questions evaluate your ability to see a problem developing or to identify an existing problem (but not necessarily solve the problem).

1. One version of this type of question tests for the ability to detect a problem in the variations of statements provided by witnesses to a crime.

2. Another version of this type of question may test your ability to see a problem that would be caused if instructions were not followed correctly, such as in the mishandling of a crime scene.

DEDUCTIVE REASONING

These questions evaluate your ability to apply regulations, procedures, or general rules to specific scenarios or to arrive at a conclusion from stated principles.

1. In one version of this type of question, a law definition or section of law is provided which you must apply to a given scenario.

2. Another version of this type of question asks you to categorize a specific case based on a classification scheme (verbal or numerical) that is provided.

3. Another version may test your ability to understand and follow rules or procedures.

INDUCTIVE REASONING

These questions evaluate your ability to identify a general rule from the specifics of a situation. Information Ordering questions evaluate a candidate's ability to put in order given rules or actions.

4. WRITTEN COMPREHENSION

These questions evaluate your ability to understand written language.

1. One version of this type of question is **understanding a written passage** that is provided, such as a narrative of the events of a crime, a section of law, or a written complaint.

2. Another version of this type of question may test your ability to **follow written instructions** that are provided.

Answer questions 1 - 3 based on the information contained in the following paragraphs.

Police Officers Juan Medina and Cheryl Johnston were on foot patrol on July 4, 2016 when at 10:15 a.m. they came upon the scene of a minor traffic accident (at 5th Avenue and 48th Street in Manhattan) that had occurred 5 minutes earlier. Officer Medina called the Police Dispatcher at 10:20 a.m. and reported that the two drivers, who were the only persons in the vehicles, did not sustain any personal injuries. One of the vehicles, the one driven by a male named William Buxton, did have minor damage to the front bumper, and the other vehicle, driven by a male named Jack Solmer, had extensive damage to the rear bumper.

Officer Juan Medina examined the driver's licenses, vehicle registration certificates and vehicle insurance identification cards. The auto driven by William Buxton, age 39, was a silver 2009 Lexus, N.Y. license plate 9327ZA, owned by the driver, residing at 2932 East 78th Street, New York, N.Y. Mr. Buxton's N.Y. driver's license identification number is D1749 38647 92132 and the expiration date is November 30, 2018.

The driver of the other auto was Jack Solmer, age 41, residing at 9822 East 7th Street, Brooklyn, N.Y. Mr. Solmer's auto was a blue 2007 Infinity, NY license plate 407PMB. Mr. Solmer's driver's license identification number is A214 295 337 and the expiration date is December 31, 2018.

Officers Medina and Johnston completed a Vehicle Accident Report at 10:35 a.m. The report number was 08492647437.

-----

1. Select the best answer: What is the time of the accident?
A. 10:15 a.m.   C. 10:20 a.m.
B. 10:35 a.m.   **D. before 10:15 a.m.**

----

2. How many persons were injured as a result of the traffic accident?
A. 1   C. 2
B. 0   D. none of the above

----

3. Which car sustained extensive damage to the rear bumper?
A. NY plate #407PMB, silver 2007 Infinity
B. NY plate #9327ZA, silver 2009 Lexus
C. NY plate #9327ZA, blue 2009 Lexus
D. NY plate #407PMB, blue 2007 Infinity

Answers 1 – 3 (Correct answers are in **bold** and **underlined**.)

1. Select the best answer: What is the time of the accident?

A. 10:15 a.m.

B. 10:35 a.m.

C. 10:20 a.m.

D. before 10:15 a.m.

("Police Officers Juan Medina and Cheryl Johnston were on foot patrol on July 4, 2016 when at 10:15 a.m. they came upon the scene of a minor traffic accident (at 5th Avenue and 48th Street in Manhattan) that had occurred 5 minutes earlier."

The traffic accident happened 5 minutes before 10:15 a.m. (the time that the officers arrived at the scene). Therefore, the accident happened at 10:10 a.m. This 10:10 a.m. time is not listed as one of the choices, and choices "B" and "C" are times after 10:15 a.m. The best choice therefore is **"D. before 10:15 a.m."**)

----

2. How many persons were injured as a result of the traffic accident?

A. 1

B. 0

C. 2

D. none of the above

(In paragraph one it states, "... the two drivers, who were the only persons in the vehicles, did not sustain any personal injuries.")

----

3. Which car sustained extensive damage to the rear bumper?

A. NY plate #407PMB, silver 2007 Infinity

B. NY plate #9327ZA, silver 2009 Lexus

C. NY plate #9327ZA, blue 2009 Lexus

D. NY plate #407PMB, blue 2007 Infinity

(In paragraph one it states, **"...the other vehicle, driven by a male named Jack Solmer, had extensive damage to the rear bumper...."** In paragraph three it states, Mr. Solmer's auto was a blue 2007 Infinity, NY license plate 407PMB." The answer is choice **"D"** and not choice "A" because in choice "A" the color of the vehicle is stated as silver.)

Answer questions 4 - 6 based on the information contained in the following paragraphs.

Police Officers Jonathan Spencer and Anita Korich were on patrol in their squad car on May 17, 2016 when at 4:47 p.m. they witnessed a traffic accident at the intersection of 13th Avenue and 39th Street in Brooklyn. Officer Spencer called the Police Dispatcher at 4:55 p.m. and reported that the two drivers and their six passengers (three in each vehicle) did not sustain any personal injuries. One of the vehicles, the one driven by a male, Clark Winston, had damage to the driver's door, and the other vehicle, driven by a female, Beverly Marino, had damage to the front bumper and right side.

Officer Korich examined the driver's licenses, vehicle registration certificates and vehicle insurance identification cards. The auto driven by Clark Winston, age 49, was a red 2010 Ford Fusion, N.Y. license plate 3374BH, owned by the driver, residing at 2532 Cadman Plaza, Brooklyn, N.Y. Mr. Winston's N.Y. driver's license identification number is M3842 48547 62537 and the expiration date is October 31, 2018.

The driver of the other auto was Beverly Marino, age 54, residing at 165 Kings Avenue, Brooklyn, N.Y. Ms. Marino's auto was a black 2008 Ford Taurus, NY license plate 5491HKD. Ms. Marino's driver's license identification number is B315 396 236 and the expiration is December 31, 2018.

Officers Spencer and Korich completed a Vehicle Accident Report at 5:35 p.m. The report number was 04495642441.

4. What is the time of the accident?
A. 4:47 a.m.   C. 5:35 p.m.
B. 5:55 p.m.   D. 4:47 p.m.

----

5. Which car sustained damage to the front bumper and right side?
A. NY plate #5497HDK, black 2008 Ford Taurus
B. NY plate #3374BH, red 2010 Ford Fusion
C. NY plate #5491HKD, black 2008 Ford Taurus
D. NY plate #3374BH, red 2001 Ford Fusion

----

6. What is the total number of persons in the two vehicles?
A. 2   C. 9
B. 6   D. none of the above

Answers 4 - 6 (Correct answers are in **bold and underlined**.)

4. What is the time of the accident?
A. 4:47 a.m.   C. 5:35 p.m.
B. 5:55 p.m.   **D. 4:47 p.m.**
(In paragraph one it states, "Police Officers Jonathan Spencer and Anita Korich were on patrol in their squad car on May 17, 2016 when at <u>4:47 p.m.</u> they witnessed a traffic accident....")

----

5. Which car sustained damage to the front bumper and right side?
A. NY plate #5497HDK, black 2008 Ford Taurus
B. NY plate #3374BH, red 2010 Ford Fusion
<u>C. NY plate #5491HKD, black 2008 Ford Taurus</u>
D. NY plate #3374BH, red 2001 Ford Fusion
(In paragraph one it states, "...the other vehicle, driven by a female, <u>Beverly Marino, had damage to the front bumper and right side.</u>" Paragraph three states, "Ms. Marino's auto was a <u>black 2008 Ford Taurus, NY license plate 5491HKD.</u>")

----

6. What is the total number of persons in the two vehicles?
A. 2   C. 9
B. 6   **<u>D. none of the above</u>**
(In paragraph one it states, "...<u>the two drivers and their six passengers</u> did not sustain any personal injuries."
(2 drivers + 6 passengers = 8 persons)
The correct answer (8) is not listed as a choice. Therefore, **"<u>D. none of the above,</u>"** is the correct choice.)

Answer questions 7 - 10 based on the information contained in the following paragraphs.

Police Officers Albert Dixon and Susan Chin were on patrol in their squad car on June 7, 2016 when at 6:35 p.m. a man approached them. The man pointed to his parked car and stated that a blue Infinity had just sideswiped it. The blue Infinity was now stopped about one hundred feet down the block. Police Officer Albert Dixon called the police dispatcher at 6:40 p.m. and reported the traffic accident (which occurred in front of 745 3rd Avenue, Staten Island). Police

Officer Susan Chin questioned the driver of the stopped blue Infinity. Both Police Officers reported to the dispatcher that the driver of the blue Infinity and the owner of the sideswiped car (a 2008 Chevy Malibu) did not sustain any injuries. Also, there were no passengers in the two cars. One of the vehicles, the blue Infinity, was driven and owned by a male, Matthew Fowler. It had damage to the front bumper. The other vehicle, owned by a male, Mark Peterson, had damage to the two doors on the driver's side.

Officer Dixon examined the driver's licenses, vehicle registration certificates and vehicle insurance identification cards. The auto driven by Matthew Fowler, age 42, was a blue 2012 Infinity, N.Y. license plate 45834DK, owned by the driver, residing at 147-49 Ferdinand Road, Brooklyn, N.Y. Mr. Fowler's N.Y. driver's license identification number is P3647 38537 22438 and the expiration date is September 30, 2018.

The owner of the parked auto was Mark Peterson, age 57, residing at 284 West 6th Street, Bronx, N.Y. Mr. Peterson's auto was a silver 2008 Chevy Malibu, NY license plate 2493GKL. Mr. Peterson's driver's license identification number is C615 792 339 and the expiration is November 30, 2018.

Officers Dixon and Chin completed a Vehicle Accident Report at 7:05 p.m. The report number was 024976454324.

----

7. Select the best answer: The time of the accident is approximately:
A. 6:35 a.m.   C. 9:40 p.m.
B. 6:53 p.m.   D) 6:35 p.m.

----

8. Which car sustained damage to the two doors on the driver's side?
A. NY plate #45834DK, blue 2012 Infinity
B. NY plate #2493GKL, silver 2008 Chevy Malibu
C. NY plate #45834DK, silver 2012 Infinity
D. NY plate #2493GKL, blue 2008 Chevy Malibu

----

9. What is the total number of persons (passengers and drivers) involved?
A. 1   C. 3
B) 2   D. none of the above

----

10. The owner of the parked vehicle resides at:
A. 284 West 6th Street, Brooklyn, NY   C. 147-49 Ferdinand Road, Brooklyn, N.Y.
B. 745 3rd Avenue, Staten Island   D. 284 West 6th Street, Bronx, N.Y.

Answers 7 – 10 (Correct answers are in **bold and underlined**.)

7. Select the best answer: The time of the accident is approximately:
A. 6:35 a.m.   C. 9:40 p.m.
B. 6:53 p.m.   **D. 6:35 p.m.**

(In paragraph one it states, "Police Officers Albert Dixon and Susan Chin were on patrol in their squad car on June 7, 2016 when at 6:35 p.m. a man approached them. The man pointed to his parked car and stated that a blue Infinity had just sideswiped it.")

----

8. Which car sustained damage to the two doors on the driver's side?
A. NY plate #45834DK, blue 2012 Infinity

B. NY plate #2493GKL, silver 2008 Chevy Malibu
C. NY plate #45834DK, silver 2012 Infinity
D. NY plate #2493GKL, blue 2008 Chevy Malibu
(In paragraph two it states, "The owner of the parked auto was Mark Peterson, age 57, residing at 284 West 6th Street, Bronx, N.Y. Mr. Peterson's auto was a <u>silver 2008 Chevy Malibu, NY license plate 2493GKL</u>.")

----

9. What is the total number of persons (passengers and drivers) involved?
A. 1   C. 3
B. 2   D. none of the above
(Only the two drivers were involved. "Both Police Officers reported to the dispatcher that the driver of the blue Infinity and the owner of the sideswiped car (a 2008 Chevy Malibu) did not sustain any injuries. Also, "...<u>there were no passengers in the two cars</u>.")

----

10. The owner of the parked vehicle resides at:
A. 284 West 6th Street, Brooklyn, NY   C. 147-49 Ferdinand Road, Brooklyn, N.Y.
B. 745 3rd Avenue, Staten Island   **D. 284 West 6th Street, Bronx, N.Y.**
(Paragraph 3: "The owner of the parked auto was Mark Peterson, age 57, residing at <u>284 West 6th Street, Bronx, NY</u>.")

Answer questions 11 - 12 based on the following:

Procedure for an Arrest on a Felony Offense

1. A person arrested for a felony offense must be handcuffed by the arresting officer.

2. The accused must be held in a police station or jail pending his or her ability to post bail in the amount set by the Judge at the first court appearance.

3. If the accused cannot post bail, the accused must be held in a secure facility.

4. If the accused posts bail, he or she must be released and ordered to appear at the next court date.

5. If the accused does not appear on the next scheduled court date, he or she forfeits any bail the Judge may have ordered and the Judge must order the issuance of an arrest warrant.

-----

11. A person arrested on a felony charge appears before the Judge in court. The Judge sets a bail of $250,000.00. The person posts the entire bail and is released and ordered by the Judge to return on a specified date. On the return date, he does not appear. Based on the above "Procedure for an Arrest on a Felony Offense," which of the following statements is correct?

A. The person must be notified to appear on the next court date or a warrant of arrest will be issued.

B. The bail must be held on deposit by the court and returned to the person when he comes to court on the next court date.

C. If a warrant of arrest is ordered by the Judge, the bail is not forfeited.

D. The bail must be forfeited and a warrant of arrest must be ordered by the Judge.

----

12. According to the "Procedure for an Arrest on a Felony Offense," which of the following statements is correct?

A. If the accused refuses to post bail, he or she must be released and ordered to appear at the next court date.

B. The accused must be held in a police station or jail pending his or her ability to post bail in the amount set by the Police Captain.

C. A person arrested for a felony must not be handcuffed.

D. The Judge must order the issuance of an arrest warrant if the accused does not appear on the next scheduled court date.

Answers 11-12

11. A person arrested on a felony charge appears before the Judge in court. The Judge sets a bail of $250,000.00. The person posts the entire bail and is released and ordered by the Judge to return on a specified date. On the return date, he does not appear. Based on the above "Procedure for an Arrest on a Felony Offense," which of the following statements is correct?

A. The person must be notified to appear on the next court date or a warrant of arrest will be issued.

(**NOT CORRECT** because bail must be forfeited and the judge must order a warrant of arrest.)

B. The bail must be held on deposit by the court and returned to the person when he comes to court on the next court date.

(**NOT CORRECT** because bail must be forfeited now and the judge must order a warrant of arrest.)

C. If a warrant of arrest is ordered by the Judge, the bail is not forfeited.

(**NOT CORRECT**. Bail is forfeited.)

D. The bail must be forfeited and a warrant of arrest must be ordered by the Judge.

(**CORRECT**. "If the accused does not appear on the next scheduled court date, he or she forfeits any bail the Judge may have ordered and the Judge must order the issuance of an arrest warrant.")

---

12. According to the "Procedure for an Arrest on a Felony Offense," which of the following statements is correct?

A. If the accused refuses to post bail, he or she must be released and ordered to appear at the next court date.

(**NOT CORRECT**. Person must _not_ be released if he does not post bail.)

B. The accused must be held in a police station or jail pending his or her ability to post bail in the amount set by the Police Captain.

(**NOT CORRECT**. Bail is set by the judge.)

C. A person arrested for a felony must not be handcuffed.

(**NOT CORRECT**. The person <u>must</u> be handcuffed.)

D. The Judge must order the issuance of an arrest warrant if the accused does not appear on the next scheduled court date.

(**CORRECT**. "If the accused does not appear on the next scheduled court date, he or she forfeits any bail the Judge may have ordered and the Judge must order the issuance of an arrest warrant.")

———————————

5. WRITTEN EXPRESSION

WRITTEN EXPRESSION questions evaluate your ability to communicate clearly and concisely in writing by using the proper words in a grammatically correct way and in a way that others will understand.

1. One version of this type of question asks you to select the **best way to communicate some thoughts or idea**s to other persons.

2. Another version of this type of question asks you to **put in a logical order four or five initially "out of order sentences"** in a sequence so that others will understand what is being communicated.

Before we attempt a written expression question, let's develop an approach to this type of question and do a quick review of some basic rules of grammar, usage, punctuation and sentence structure.

FIRST, READ EACH SELECTION CAREFULLY TO SEE IF IT HAS ANY OF THE FOLLOWING FLAWS:

1. DOES IT SOUND LIKE ENGLISH - OR DOES IT SOUND LIKE STREET TALK?
Some obvious examples: (Underlining is for emphasis of correct/incorrect English usage.)
>**Correct:** I <u>go</u> to the store every day.
>**Not Correct:** I <u>goes</u> to the store every day.

>**Correct:** It <u>doesn't</u> matter how much it costs.
>**Not Correct:** It <u>don't</u> matter how much it costs.

2. IS THE SENTENCE IN A LOGICAL SEQUENCE? ARE THE MAIN IDEAS PROPERLY CONNECTED?
Example: Which of the following three choices is/are correct?
>(1) The boy who dropped out of high school didn't like to study.
>(2) The boy didn't like to study dropped out of high school.
>(3) The boy dropped out didn't like to study.
Answer: (1) is the most logical and grammatically correct.

3. ARE THERE ANY MISSPELLED WORDS?
Example:
>assistant and NOT asistant
>court facility and NOT court fasility
>believe and NOT beleive

precinct and NOT precint
(For a list of important spelling and vocabulary words, see section 12.)

4. ARE WORDS USED CORRECTLY?

The principal (NOT principle) of the school was Mr. Kane.
The advice (NOT advise) was very welcomed.
They complimented (NOT complemented) her for her hard work.
Their (NOT there) car needed repair.
He picked up the stationery (NOT stationary) for the captain in room 605.
He was too (NOT "to" or "two") happy to speak.
The Police Officer accepted (NOT excepted) the medal.
The work site (NOT cite) was very clean.
Someone who is not moving is stationary (NOT stationery).
The capital city (NOT capitol) of New York State is Albany.

5. ARE APOSTROPHES USED CORRECTLY?

The boy's (NOT boys) hat was yellow.

IF YOU CANNOT ELIMINATE THE SELECTION AS BEING BAD AFTER APPLYING THE ABOVE GENERAL RULES, REVIEW THE SELECTION FOR THE FOLLOWING GRAMMATICAL ERRORS. (REMEMBER THAT FOR ALL THE FOLLOWING RULES, THERE ARE EXCEPTIONS.)

1. EVERY SENTENCE BEGINS WITH A CAPITAL LETTER AND ENDS WITH A PERIOD.

2. FOR A SENTENCE TO BE COMPLETE, IT MUST HAVE AT MINIMUM A SUBJECT AND A PREDICATE. OTHERWISE, IT IS JUST A SENTENCE FRAGMENT.

A **subject** is usually a noun (person, place, or thing) about which something is asked or stated. Example: The police officer (subject) speaks softly.

A **predicate** contains a verb (an "action" word) and is the part of the sentence about what is said about the subject. In the above example, the predicate is "speaks."

3. A VERB AND ITS SUBJECT MUST AGREE IN NUMBER.
The Police Officers <u>looks</u> tall. (NOT CORRECT)
The Police Officers <u>look</u> tall. (CORRECT)
Police Officers is plural (more than one). "Police Officers" and "look" agree in number.

Another example:
The men and the woman <u>works</u> in the same precinct. (NOT CORRECT)
The men and the woman <u>work</u> in the same precinct. (CORRECT)

The men and the woman is a plural subject and takes a plural verb <u>work</u>.

The boy <u>works</u> (singular verb). The boy and girl <u>work</u> (plural verb).

4. A COMMA USUALLY GOES BEFORE THE FOLLOWING WORDS - but, for, or, nor, so, yet - WHEN THE WORD CONNECTS TWO MAIN CLAUSES.
Examples:
He didn't like to study, but he liked to play.

He scored a high mark, for he had received good training.
You can try hard and succeed, or you can make a feeble attempt and fail.
He didn't try hard, nor did he try for long.
He studied long and hard, so he passed.
He was sick when he took the test, yet he did very well.

5. A COMMA USUALLY GOES AFTER AN INTRODUCTORY PHRASE.
Examples:
When you study, you build up the neural connections in your brain.
Because of hard work and a little good luck, he succeeded in life.

6. A COMMA USUALLY GOES BETWEEN SEPARATE ITEMS IN A LIST OR SERIES OF ADJECTIVES.
Examples:
The boy was young, proud, and happy.
The tall, young, proud boy walked up to the front of the room.

7. COMMAS USUALLY SET OFF PARENTHETICAL ELEMENTS.
Examples:
Young boys, as Abraham Lincoln once observed, should not be afraid to work hard.
American soldiers, generally speaking, are very well trained.

8. A SEMICOLON IS USUALLY USED BETWEEN MAIN CLAUSES NOT LINKED BY and, but, for, or, nor, so, yet.
Examples:
The young boys played basketball; the older men sat on the bleachers.
The war had many battles; few were as fierce as this one.
(Notice that the letter after the semicolon is NOT capitalized.)

9. THE COLON IS USUALLY USED TO DIRECT ATTENTION TO A SERIES.
Example:
The ingredients of success are as follows: hard work, commitment, and luck.

If grammar is not your strong point, or if you feel you need to concentrate more on it, there are many "rules of grammar" books available. For free online resources, search "rules of grammar" for an almost endless number of informative websites.

(For a list of important spelling and vocabulary words, see section 12.

Questions 1-5

1. The owner of Johnson's Grocery Shop at the Midland Rest Stop informs Trooper Miler that ten minutes earlier he noticed two cartons of cigarettes missing from his display, right after a biker and his girlfriend who had been shopping left the store. The store owner had followed them outside. However, they sped away north on their motorcycle before he was able to ask them about the missing cigarettes. Trooper Miller wishes to report this. The most effective way for Trooper Miller to summarize the facts is:

A. Ten minutes ago, the owner of Johnson's Grocery Shop at the Midland Rest Stop said that he found two cartons of cigarettes missing from his display, right after a couple of bikers left the store and sped away north.

(B.) The owner of Johnson's Grocery Shop at the Midland Rest Stop said that ten minutes ago, he discovered two cartons of cigarettes missing from his display, right after a male and female biker left the store and sped away north on their motorcycle.

C. Two cartons of cigarettes are missing from the Midland Rest Stop. The suspects are two bikers that are heading north.

D. Two bikers heading north must be arrested. They stole two cartons of cigarettes from Johnson's Grocery Store at the Midland Rest Stop.

----

2. Officer Parker is scheduled to give a speech at a local civic association regarding the distinction between emergency number 911 and general public information and assistance number 311, including when to properly use each number. He wishes to stress the valuable public assistance resources that can be accessed using 311 and the emergency assistance that is provided by calling 911. At the end of his presentation he wishes to include a statement which summarizes these facts. Based on this goal, which of the following choices is the best statement that he should use?

A. Please keep in mind that the aim of both numbers is to provide assistance to all the public, regardless of age, gender, or nationality.

B. In an emergency, call either 911 or 311. Both numbers will be answered by trained personnel who will do their best to assist you.

(C) Please keep in mind that 911 should be used for emergency situations. If you need non-emergency information, including access to public assistance resources, please call 311.

D. Please call 311 for any emergency situation. In the alternative, you may call 911 if you wish.

----

3. Organize the following five sentences in the best logical order.
1. Because of this, he called 911 and reported the fire.
2. The firemen put the fire out and the police arrested the suspect, while he was still holding the gasoline canister.
3. In less than three minutes, both the police and a firetruck arrived on the scene.
4. A pedestrian reported that he witnessed the suspect entering the dark alley with a gasoline canister.
5. A minute later flames erupted in the alley, behind the Melrose Center Bank.

A. 4, 2, 3, 5, 1   C. 3, 4, 2, 1, 5
B. 5, 4, 3, 1, 2   (D.) 4, 5, 1, 3, 2

----

4. For the past three months, you have been assigned at the gated entrance of a NYS enterprise zone, and followed this authorized procedure: You randomly checked the Enterprise Zone I.D. cards of incoming individuals in cars. You asked drivers of those incoming vehicles to produce a driver's license, registration, and proof of insurance. If the driver was transporting alcohol, you asked for identification that proved the driver was of legal age to drink. If proper I.D. was not produced or if the driver was below the legal age to drink alcohol, you informed the private security staff.

Because of your reassignment to the Albany Administrative Center, you are asked to convey the above procedure to three Troopers that will be assigned to the enterprise zone. Which of the following choices best conveys the enterprise zone procedure that you followed?

A. Check the Enterprise Zone I.D. cards of incoming individuals in cars. Ask the drivers of incoming vehicles to show their driver's license, registration, and proof of insurance. If the driver is transporting alcohol, ask for I.D. that proves that the occupants of the car are of legal age to drink. If proper I.D. is not produced or if the driver is below the legal age to drink alcohol, inform the private security staff.

B. Check all cars for alcohol, and check the drivers' I.D. Any problems, report them to the private security staff.

C. Your job is to make sure that all I.D. is proper and that there is no alcohol in the cars. Any problems, contact the private security staff and have them proceed.

D. At the gated entrance, stop cars on a random basis and check the I.D. of drivers (and driver's license, registration and proof of insurance). The driver must be of legal age to drink (if there is alcohol in the car). If the driver is below the legal age, or if proper I.D. is not produced, inform the private security staff.

----

5. Officer Ahren is asked to select the best summary (A, B, C, or D) of the following information: (The best summary is the one that expresses the information in the **most clear, accurate and complete manner**).

Place of accident: in front of 1726 West 8th Street, Brooklyn
Time of accident: 12:25 P.M.
Date of accident: September 11, 2016
Vehicle involved: 2006 Toyota
Driver: Cecilia Langer
Damage: cracked windshield
Details: A small branch fell from a tree and cracked the windshield of a 2006 Toyota.

A. On September 11, 2016, in front of 1726 West 8th Street, Brooklyn, a small branch fell from a tree and cracked the windshield of a 2006 Toyota, owned by Cecilia Langer.

B. On September 11, 2016, in front of 1726 West 8th Street, Brooklyn, a small branch fell from a tree and cracked the windshield of a 2006 Toyota, driven by Cecilia Langer.

C. On September 11, 2016, at 12:52 P.M., in front of 1726 West 8th Street, Brooklyn, a small branch fell from a tree and cracked the windshield of a 2006 Toyota, driven by Cecilia Langer.

D. On September 11, 2016, at 12:25 P.M., in front of 1726 West 8th Street, Brooklyn, a small branch fell from a tree and cracked the windshield of a 2006 Toyota, driven by Cecilia Langer.

Answers 1-5

1. The owner of Johnson's Grocery Shop at the Midland Rest Stop informs Trooper Miler that ten minutes earlier he noticed two cartons of cigarettes missing from his display, right after a biker and his girlfriend who had been shopping left the store. The store owner had followed them outside. However, they sped away north on their motorcycle before he was able to ask them about the missing cigarettes. Trooper Miller wishes to report this. The most effective way for Trooper Miller to summarize the facts is:

A. Ten minutes ago, the owner of Johnson's Grocery Shop at the Midland Rest Stop said that he found two cartons of cigarettes missing from his display, right after a couple of bikers left the store and sped away north.

(**This is the NOT the best choice.** The owner of the store reported the incident now and not ten minutes ago. The "couple of bikers" does not specify that one was male and one was female. Also, it does not specify that they sped away on a motorcycle and not on a bicycle.)

B. The owner of Johnson's Grocery Shop at the Midland Rest Stop said that ten minutes ago he discovered two cartons of cigarettes missing from his display, right after a male and female biker left the store and sped away north on their motorcycle.

(**This is the CORRECT ANSWER.** All the facts are included in a clear and concise manner.)

C. Two cartons of cigarettes are missing from the Midland Rest Stop. The suspects are two bikers that are heading north.

(**This is NOT the best choice.** It is too sketchy and leaves out important details, such as when the event occurred and the name of the store. It also uses confusing words such as "bikers" which may mean people on bicycles or on motorcycles.)

D. Two bikers heading north must be arrested. They stole two cartons of cigarettes from Johnson's Grocery Store at the Midland Rest Stop.

(**This is NOT the best choice**. It states flatly that the bikers stole the cartons. However, at this point they are just suspects. Also, it leaves out details such as the time of the incident and the genders of the bikers.)

----

2. Officer Parker is scheduled to give a speech at a local civic association regarding the distinction between emergency number 911 and general public information and assistance number 311, including when to properly use each number. He wishes to stress the valuable public assistance resources that can be accessed using 311 and the emergency assistance that is provided by calling 911. At the end of his presentation he wishes to include a statement which summarizes these facts. Based on this goal, which of the following choices is the best statement that he should use?

A. Please keep in mind that the aim of both numbers is to provide assistance to all the public, regardless of age, gender, or nationality.

(**This is not the best choice.** Although the statement is true, it does not address the aim of Officer Parker, which is to convey the emergency nature of 911, and the non-emergency nature of 311.)

B. In an emergency, call either 911 or 311. Both numbers will be answered by trained personnel who will do their best to assist you.

(**This is not the best choice.** Again, it does not address the aim of Officer Parker, which is to convey the emergency nature of 911, and the non-emergency nature of 311.)

C. Please keep in mind that 911 should be used for emergency situations. If you need non-emergency information, including access to public assistance resources, please call 311.
(**This is the best choice.** The statement clearly expresses the message which Officer Parker wishes to convey.)

D. Please call 311 for any emergency situation. In the alternative, you may call 911 if you wish. (**This is not the best choice.** This statement is not factual and suggests incorrect usage of the two numbers.)

----

3. Organize the following five sentences in the best logical order.
1. Because of this, he called 911 and reported the fire.
2. The firemen put the fire out and the police arrested the suspect, while he was still holding the gasoline canister.
3. In less than three minutes, both the police and a firetruck arrived on the scene.
4. A pedestrian reported that he witnessed the suspect entering the dark alley with a gasoline canister.
5. A minute later flames erupted in the alley, behind the Melrose Center Bank.

A. 4, 2, 3, 5, 1
B. 5, 4, 3, 1, 2
C. 3, 4, 2, 1, 5
D. 4, 5, 1, 3, 2

Answer is **D. 4, 5, 1, 3, 2**
4. A pedestrian reported that he witnessed the suspect entering the dark alley with a gasoline canister.
5. A minute later flames erupted in the alley, behind the Melrose Center Bank.
1. Because of this, he called 911 and reported the fire.
3. In less than three minutes, both the police and a firetruck arrived on the scene.
2. The firemen put the fire out and the police arrested the suspect, while he was still holding the gasoline canister.

----

4. For the past three months, you have been assigned at the gated entrance of a NYS enterprise zone, and followed this authorized procedure: You randomly checked the Enterprise Zone I.D. cards of incoming individuals in cars. You asked drivers of those incoming vehicles to produce a driver's license, registration, and proof of insurance. If the driver was transporting alcohol, you asked for identification that proved the driver was of legal age to drink. If proper I.D. was not produced or if the driver was below the legal age to drink alcohol, you informed the private security staff.

Because of your reassignment to the Albany Administrative Center, you are asked to convey the above procedure to three Troopers that will be assigned to the enterprise zone. Which of the following choices best conveys the enterprise zone procedure that you followed?

A. Check the Enterprise Zone I.D. cards of incoming individuals in cars. Ask the drivers of incoming vehicles to show their driver's license, registration, and proof of insurance. If the driver is transporting alcohol, ask for I.D. that proves that the occupants of the car are of legal age to drink. If proper I.D. is not produced or if the driver is below the legal age to drink alcohol, inform the private security staff.

(**This is not the best choice.** It does not state that the checking of the Enterprise Zone I.D. cards should be done on a <u>random</u> basis. Also, the procedure does <u>not</u> require that <u>all the occupants of the car</u> be of legal drinking age (only the driver.))

B. Check all cars for alcohol, and check the drivers' I.D. Any problems, report them to the private security staff.

(**This is not the best choice.** It is too sketchy. It leaves out the randomness of the search, the legal age to drink, and the details about what documents are to be produced by the driver.)

C. Your job is to make sure that all I.D. is proper and that there is no alcohol in the cars. Any problems, contact the private security staff and have them proceed.

(**This is not the best choice**. It misstates the duties and is missing much of the required details.)

D. At the gated entrance, stop cars on a random basis and check the I.D. of drivers (and driver's license, registration and proof of insurance). The driver must be of legal age to drink (if there is alcohol in the car). If the driver is below the legal age, or if proper I.D. is not produced, inform the private security staff.

(**This is the best choice**. All the required information is present, and the statement is clear.)

----

5. Officer Ahren is asked to select the best summary (A, B, C, or D) of the following information: (The best summary is the one that expresses the information in the **most clear, accurate and complete manner**).

Place of accident: in front of 1726 West 8th Street, Brooklyn

Time of accident: 12:25 P.M.

Date of accident: September 11, 2016

Vehicle involved: 2006 Toyota

Driver: Cecilia Langer

Damage: cracked windshield

Details: A small branch fell from a tree and cracked the windshield of a 2006 Toyota.

A. On September 11, 2016, in front of 1726 West 8th Street, Brooklyn, a small branch fell from a tree and cracked the windshield of a 2006 Toyota, <u>owned</u> by Cecilia Langer.

(**WRONG** because it states the car was "<u>owned</u>" by Cecilia Langer. The information says that Cecilia Langer was the "<u>driver</u>." Also, the time of the accident, 12:25 P.M., is not stated.)

B. On September 11, 2016, in front of 1726 West 8th Street, Brooklyn, a small branch fell from a tree and cracked the windshield of a 2006 Toyota, driven by Cecilia Langer.

(**WRONG** because the time of the accident, 12:25 P.M. is not stated.)

C. On September 11, 2016, at 12:52 P.M., in front of 1726 West 8th Street, Brooklyn, a small branch fell from a tree and cracked the windshield of a 2006 Toyota, driven by Cecilia Langer.

(**WRONG** because the time of the accident is wrong. The correct time is <u>12:25</u> P.M. and not <u>12:52</u> P.M.)

D. On September 11, 2016, at 12:25 P.M., in front of 1726 West 8th Street, Brooklyn, a small branch fell from a tree and cracked the windshield of a 2006 Toyota, driven by Cecilia Langer.

(**CORRECT ANSWER.** This is the only choice that contains all the information and does not contain any factual errors.)

_____

Questions 6-10

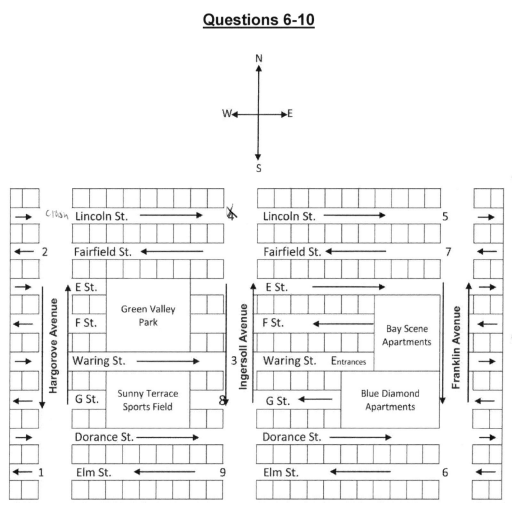

6. You are in the passenger seat of a patrol car driving south and you are at the intersection of Lincoln St. and Ingersoll Avenue. You are informed that a major auto accident has just occurred at the intersection of Lincoln St. and Hargrove Avenue. Since the officer who is driving is not familiar with the area, you must provide directions to the accident site. Assuming that you must obey all traffic signs, which one of the following four choices clearly describes the most direct route?

A. Drive straight west to the intersection of Lincoln St. and Hargrove Avenue, one block away.

B. Drive east to Franklin Avenue, then south on Franklin Avenue to Fairfield Street, then west on Fairfield St. to Hargrove Avenue, then north on Hargrove Avenue to the intersection of Lincoln St. and Hargrove Avenue.

C. Drive straight east to the intersection of Lincoln St. and Hargrove Avenue, one block away.

D. Drive south on Ingersoll Avenue to Fairfield St, then drive west on Fairfield St. to Hargrove Avenue, then north to the intersection of Lincoln St. and Hargrove Avenue.

----

7. Trooper Jane Davidson has been asked by her Sergeant to discuss with new Troopers the duties of the Troopers, the policies of her unit, and proper dress, especially the beneficial effect on their daily assignments of a professional and well-groomed appearance. The duties will include patrolling specified areas, and may also include brief assignments in the administrative office. One of the policies of her unit is the rotation of week-end assignments. She is also to cover the policy of volunteering to cover the duties of a Trooper with any family emergencies. Trooper Davidson estimates that her talk will last about ten minutes and cover a wide range of information. Because of this, she wishes to make sure that at the end of the speech she stresses what her Sergeant requested her to emphasize.

Based on the preceding, which of the following choices best expresses what Trooper Davidson and her Sergeant wish to stress?

A. Covering for our fellow Troopers is important in their time of need.

B. Troopers that do not adhere to the policies and units will have official counseling reports placed in their files.

C. All policies and rules are important and must be adhered to.

D. A well-groomed appearance and a professional demeanor are important in carrying out our daily duties.

----

8. Organize the following four sentences in the best logical order:

1. This training includes classroom and "on the street" practice driving.

2. Because of this, they receive proper driving and safety instruction.

3. "On the street" driving is stressed and comprises eighty percent of the training time.

4. New York State Troopers may be assigned to drive a highway emergency vehicle.

(A) 1, 3, 4, 2

(B) 2, 3, 4, 1

(C) 3, 2, 1, 4

(D) 4, 2, 1, 3

----

9. You are asked to convey the following procedure to three Troopers that have been assigned to your area of responsibility. "The overtime policy is uniform and applied fairly in all cases. First, whether to work overtime is not at the discretion of New York State employees. It may be mandated when necessary and other suitable volunteer employees are not available to perform the work during the overtime period. Although certain duties may be performed by employees in any job title, some duties must be performed only by employees in designated job titles. An example of this may be found in the staffing of magnetometer posts. Although New York State Troopers routinely staff them, in the absence of sufficient New York State personnel of this title, other employees who are trained in magnetometer operation and who, like New York State Troopers are police officers, may operate the magnetometers."

Which of the following choices correctly conveys important facts regarding overtime?

A. All New York State employees may operate magnetometers on an overtime basis, when necessary, and must do so, if necessary.

B. Because of their important role in enforcing the laws, New York State Troopers receive a preference if they wish to work overtime in any agency.

C. If there are sufficient New York State Troopers available, they receive a preference in the staffing of magnetometer posts on overtime.

D. Because overtime is applied fairly, all employees must place their names on the "Requested Overtime List."

----

10. New York State Trooper Slavik obtains the following information at the scene of a traffic accident:

Date of accident: July 4, 2016

Time of accident: 2:25 P.M.

Place of accident: intersection of 5th Avenue and 48th Street, Staten Island

Vehicles involved: 2007 Nissan and 2011 Buick

Drivers: Abe Molson (2007 Nissan) and Carol Soto (2011 Buick)

Damage: dent on driver's door of 2011 Buick

Trooper Slavik drafts four versions to express the above information. Which of the following four versions is most clear, accurate and complete?

A. On July 4, 2016, at 2:25 P.M., at the intersection of 5th Avenue and 48th Street, Staten Island, a 2007 Nissan and a 2011 Buick were involved in a traffic accident. The 2011 Buick, owned by Carol Soto, sustained a dent on the driver's door. The 2007 Nissan, driven by Abe Molson, did not sustain any damage.

B. At the intersection of 5th Avenue and 48th Street, Staten Island, a 2007 Nissan, owned by Abe Molson, and a 2011 Buick owned by Carol Soto, were involved in a car accident. The driver's door of the 2007 Nissan was dented. The accident occurred on July 4, 2016, at 2:25 P.M.

C. At the intersection of 5th Avenue and 48th Street, a 2007 Buick, owned by Abe Molson, and a 2011 Buick owned by Carol Soto, were involved in a car accident. The driver's door of the 2007 Nissan was dented. The accident occurred on July 4, 2016.

D. On July 4, 2016, at 2:25 P.M., at the intersection of 5th Avenue and 48th Street, Staten Island, a 2007 Nissan and a 2011 Buick were involved in a traffic accident. The 2011 Buick, driven by Carol Soto, sustained a dent on the driver's door. The 2007 Nissan, driven by Abe Molson, did not sustain any damage.

Answer 6

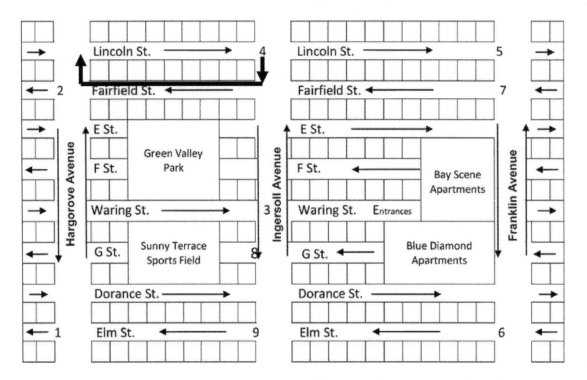

You are in the passenger seat of a patrol car driving south and you are at the intersection of Lincoln St. and Ingersoll Avenue. You are informed that a major auto accident has just occurred at the intersection of Lincoln St. and Hargrove Avenue. Since the officer who is driving is not familiar with the area, you must provide directions to the accident site. Assuming that you must obey all traffic signs, which one of the following four choices clearly describes the most direct route?

A. Drive straight west to the intersection of Lincoln St. and Hargrove Avenue, one block away.

B. Drive east to Franklin Avenue, then south on Franklin Avenue to Fairfield Street, then west on Fairfield St. to Hargrove Avenue, then north on Hargrove Avenue to the intersection of Lincoln St. and Hargrove Avenue.

C. Drive straight east to the intersection of Lincoln St. and Hargrove Avenue, one block away.

D. Drive south on Ingersoll Avenue to Fairfield St, then drive west on Fairfield St. to Hargrove Avenue, then north to the intersection of Lincoln St. and Hargrove Avenue.

(See the above map.)

Answer 7

Trooper Jane Davidson has been asked by her Sergeant to discuss with new Troopers the duties of the Troopers, the policies of her unit, and proper dress, especially the beneficial effect on their daily assignments of a professional and well-groomed appearance. The duties will include patrolling specified areas, and may also include brief assignments in the administrative office. One of the policies of her unit is the rotation of week-end assignments. She is also to cover the policy of volunteering to cover the duties of a Trooper with any family emergencies.

Trooper Davidson estimates that her talk will last about ten minutes and cover a wide range of information. Because of this, she wishes to make sure that at the end of the speech she stresses what her Sergeant requested her to emphasize.

Based on the preceding, which of the following choices best expresses what Trooper Davidson and her Sergeant wish to stress?

A. Covering for our fellow Troopers is important in their time of need.

B. Troopers that do not adhere to the policies and units will have official counseling reports placed in their files.

C. All policies and rules are important and must be adhered to.

D. A well-groomed appearance and a professional demeanor are important in carrying out our daily duties.
(This is the best choice because it stresses what her Sergeant wished to stress, the "beneficial effect on their daily assignments of a professional and well-groomed appearance."

Answer 8

Organize the following four sentences in the best logical order:

1. This training includes classroom and "on the street" practice driving.

2. Because of this, they receive proper driving and safety instruction.

3. "On the street" driving is stressed and comprises eighty percent of the training time.

4. Sanitation Workers may be assigned to drive a waste collection vehicle.

(A) 1, 3, 4, 2

(B) 2, 3, 4, 1

(C) 3, 2, 1, 4

(D) 4, 2, 1, 3

The correct answer is (D) 4, 2, 1, 3.

4. New York State Troopers may be assigned to drive a highway emergency vehicle.

(This sentence introduces the topic of driving highway emergency vehicles.)

2. Because of this, they receive proper driving and safety instruction.

1. This training includes classroom and "on the street" practice driving.

3. "On the street" driving is stressed and comprises eighty percent of the training time.

Answer 9

You are asked to convey the following procedure to three Troopers that have been assigned to your area of responsibility. "The overtime policy is uniform and applied fairly in all cases. First, whether to work overtime is not at the discretion of New York State employees. It may be mandated when necessary and other suitable volunteer employees are not available to perform the work during the overtime period. Although certain duties may be performed by employees in any job title, some duties must be performed only by employees in designated job titles. An example of this may be found in the staffing of magnetometer posts. Although

New York State Troopers routinely staff them, in the absence of sufficient New York State personnel of this title, other employees who are trained in magnetometer operation and who, like New York State Troopers are police officers, may operate the magnetometers.

Which of the following choices best conveys important facts regarding overtime?

A. All New York State employees may operate magnetometers on an overtime basis, when necessary, and must do so, if necessary.
(**This is not the best choice.** It incorrectly states that all employees may operate magnetometers.)

B. Because of their important role in enforcing the laws, New York State Troopers receive a preference if they wish to work overtime in any agency.
(**This is not the best choice.** Overtime is applied fairly in all cases, and it is only in magnetometer operation that they receive a preference because of their duties and training.)

C. If there are sufficient New York State Troopers available, they receive a preference in the staffing of magnetometer posts on overtime.
(**This is the best choice.** It correctly states that New York State Troopers routinely staff magnetometer posts.)

D. Because overtime is applied fairly, all employees must place their names on the "Requested Overtime List."
(**This is not the best choice.** The passage does not refer to any "Requested Overtime List."

Answer 10

New York State Trooper Slavik obtains the following information at the scene of a traffic accident:

Date of accident: July 4, 2016

Time of accident: 2:25 P.M.

Place of accident: intersection of 5th Avenue and 48th Street, Staten Island

Vehicles involved: 2007 Nissan and 2011 Buick

Drivers: Abe Molson (2007 Nissan) and Carol Soto (2011 Buick)

Damage: dent on driver's door of 2011 Buick

Trooper Slavik drafts four versions to express the above information. Which of the following four versions is most clear, accurate and complete?

A. On July 4, 2016, at 2:25 P.M., at the intersection of 5th Avenue and 48th Street, Staten Island, a 2007 Nissan and a 2011 Buick were involved in a traffic accident. The 2011 Buick, owned by Carol Soto, sustained a dent on the driver's door. The 2007 Nissan, driven by Abe Molson, did not sustain any damage.
(**WRONG.** This summary is not accurate. The 2011 Buick was driven by Carol Soto, not owned by her.)

B. At the intersection of 5th Avenue and 48th Street, Staten Island, a 2007 Nissan, owned by Abe Molson, and a 2011 Buick owned by Carol Soto, were involved in a car accident. The driver's door of the 2007 Nissan was dented. The accident occurred on July 4, 2016, at 2:25 P.M.

(WRONG. This summary is not accurate. The damage was to the 2011 Buick, not the 2007 Nissan. Also, the 2011 Buick was <u>driven</u> by Carol Soto, not <u>owned</u> by her, and the 2007 Nissan was <u>driven</u> by Abe Molson and not <u>owned</u> by him.)

C. At the intersection of 5th Avenue and 48th Street, a 2007 Buick, owned by Abe Molson, and a 2011 Buick owned by Carol Soto, were involved in a car accident. The driver's door of the 2007 Nissan was dented. The accident occurred on July 4, 2016.
(WRONG. This summary is incomplete and not accurate. The time of the accident, 2:25 P.M., is not stated. Also, the cars were <u>"driven by"</u> and not <u>"owned"</u> by the persons named.)

D. On July 4, 2016, at 2:25 P.M., at the intersection of 5th Avenue and 48th Street, Staten Island, a 2007 Nissan and a 2011 Buick were involved in a traffic accident. The 2011 Buick, driven by Carol Soto, sustained a dent on the driver's door. The 2007 Nissan, driven by Abe Molson, did not sustain any damage.
(CORRECT ANSWER. It contains all the information and has no errors.)

---

6. PROBLEM SENSITIVITY

These questions evaluate your ability to see a problem developing or to identify an existing problem (but not necessarily solve the problem).

1. One version of this type of question tests for the ability to detect a problem in the **variations of statements provided by witnesses** (including descriptions of persons) to a crime.

2. Another version of this type of question may test your ability to see a **problem that would be caused if instructions were not followe**d correctly, such as in the mishandling of a crime scene.

Answer question 1 based on the following "Miranda Warning."
Miranda Warning
"You have the right to remain silent when questioned.

Anything you say or do may be used against you in a court of law.

You have the right to consult an attorney before speaking to the police and to have an attorney present during questioning now or in the future.

If you cannot afford an attorney, one will be appointed for you before any questioning, if you wish.

If you decide to answer any questions now, without an attorney present, you will still have the right to stop answering at any time until you talk to an attorney.

Knowing and understanding your rights as I have explained them to you, are you willing to answer my questions without an attorney present?"

-----

1. According to the above version of the Miranda Warning, which of the following four actions by Trooper James Perkins is the most serious error?

A. Trooper Perkins asks the person being warned if he/she is willing to answer any questions without an attorney present after the person knows and understands his/her rights as explained.

B. Trooper Perkins informs the person that anything the person says or does may be used against the person in a court of law.

C. Trooper Perkins informs the person that if the person cannot afford an attorney, one will be appointed only at the time of trial.

D. Trooper Perkins informs the person that a person without an attorney present has the right to stop answering at any time until the person talks to an attorney.

Answer Question 2 and 3 based on the following Penal Law S 240.40: Appearance in public under the influence of narcotics or a drug other than alcohol, and Criminal Procedure Law (CPL) S 160.10 When fingerprints may or must be taken

Penal Law (PL) S 240.40 Appearance in public under the influence of narcotics or a drug other than alcohol.

A person is guilty of appearance in public under the influence of narcotics or a drug other than alcohol when he appears in a public place under the influence of narcotics or a drug other than alcohol to the degree that he may endanger himself or other persons or property, or annoy persons in his vicinity. Appearance in public under the influence of narcotics or a drug other than alcohol is a violation.

Criminal Procedure Law (CPL) S 160.10 When fingerprints may or must be taken

Following an arrest, or following arraignment upon a local criminal court accusatory instrument, a defendant must be fingerprinted where the accusatory instrument charges:

(a) a felony

(b) a misdemeanor defined in the Penal Law

(c) a misdemeanor defined outside of the Penal Law which would constitute a felony if such person had a previous judgment of conviction for a crime

(d) loitering for the purposes of engaging in a prostitution offense (Penal Law 240.37)

After an arrest for any offense, fingerprints may be taken where:

(a) law enforcement is unable to ascertain the person's identity.

(b) identification given by such person may not be accurate.

(c) there is reasonable cause to believe the person might be sought by law enforcement officials for the commission of some other offense.

When fingerprints are required to be taken, photographs and palm prints may be taken.

-----

2. NYS State Trooper Marino arrests a person whom he reasonably believes is appearing in public under the influence of narcotics or a drug other than alcohol and who is annoying persons in his vicinity. The person provides acceptable I.D. (NYS issued driver's license with photo).

Which of the following actions by Trooper Marino is not an error?

A. Trooper Marino causes fingerprints to be taken because the person was arrested for an offense.

B. Trooper Marino causes photographs and palm prints to be taken because they must be taken whenever fingerprints are taken.

C. Trooper Marino causes fingerprints to be taken because all drug offenses are felonies.

D. Trooper Marino prevents fingerprints to be taken because CPL S 160.10 does not authorize the taking of fingerprints in this particular instance.

3.Trooper Janet Yaeger arrests a person for loitering for the purposes of engaging in a prostitution offense (Penal Law 240.37).

Which of the following actions by Trooper Yaeger is not a serious error?

A. She directs that fingerprints not be taken if the person is under the age of 18.

B. She informs the officer taking fingerprints that fingerprints can only be taken if photographs and palm prints are also taken.

C. She directs that fingerprints must be taken, even though Officer Yaeger personally knows the identity of the person arrested, who happens to be her next-door neighbor.

D. She informs the fingerprint officer that photographs and palm prints must be taken in all cases.

Question 4-5
Crime Scene General Procedure

1. Quickly estimate the general area of the scene and determine the specific area to be secured for investigation.

2. If medical and other responders are on the scene, advise them of the requirement that evidence be preserved.

3. Establish security and permit access or exit to only authorized persons and equipment.

4. Develop a theory regarding the type of criminal offense that occurred and proceed with that in mind as you conduct a preliminary survey and walkthrough.

5. Document the scene as per Procedure CSI-265(2017).

6. Preserve all evidence and record the evidence, as per EDCI-337(2014).

7. Area security and restricted access may only be withdrawn upon written authorization, form UARF-1867(2015).

-----

4. Trooper Sampson is the second Trooper to arrive at a suspected crime scene in a rest area building where a person is found dead on the floor. The first Trooper to arrive was Trooper Fuller. Trooper Sampson quickly reviews the actions taken by Trooper Fuller. Which of the following actions by Trooper Fuller is not in accordance with the above "Crime Scene General Procedure"?

A. Trooper Fuller documented the scene as per Procedure CSI-265(2017).

B. After Trooper Fuller received authorization as per form UARF-1867(2015), he withdrew security from the scene and allowed unrestricted access.

C. Trooper Fuller only allowed access to the scene by authorized persons and equipment.

D. Trooper Fuller did not review any of the actions taken by medical personnel that arrived on the scene, even if they interfered with evidence collection, because he did not want to get in the way of medical treatments.

----

5. Which of the following four choices in not in accordance with the above "Crime Scene General Procedure."?

A. Preserve all evidence and record the evidence, as per EDCI-337(2014).

B. Establish security and permit access or exit to only authorized persons and equipment.

C. Preserve all evidence and record the evidence, as per EDCI-337(2014).

D. Document the scene as per Procedure CSI-256(2017).

Question 6

During a city marathon, one of the participants was robbed by a spectator. Four runners stated that they witnessed the robbery. The four runners voluntarily described the suspects with the following statements.

Runner 1: There were two of them, one male and one female, both wearing light jackets. The guy was around 5'10" and the woman was about 5'6". He was muscular, but she looked very slender. Both were wearing blue jeans. His were dark and hers were light. They had on white sneakers and no glasses. He was probably around 190 pounds. She was probably around 125 pounds.

Runner 2: A man and a woman did the robbery. The guy was big and she was the skinny, shorter type. He was about 5'9". I think he had dark hair and she had dirty blonde hair. Both were wearing some type of thin jackets, the windbreaker type, and blue jeans. I would say he was about 170-180 pounds. She was probably around 120-140 pounds. I didn't notice the shoes.

Runner 3: The guy was medium size, like the woman. She had dark hair, not too long, and he had brown or black hair. They were both wearing sneakers, white, I think. They were about the same height, and they were wearing khaki colored pants. I think they were both wearing sweaters.

Runner 4: I didn't get a very good look at them, but one was a guy and one was a woman. They were both under 6 feet, and she was about five inches shorter than him. She was a blonde. I think he had dark brown hair. What I remember most is their thin jackets. I think both jackets had some type of logo on the front chest pocket.

Trooper Frank Perez is assigned to review the statements of the four witnesses. Based on the preceding information supplied by the four witnesses, Officer Perez should conclude that there is a problem with the description that was provided by witness number:

A. 1   C. 3

B. 2   D. 4

Question 7

At an official NYS governmental function, a woman notified a NYS Officer that she had been pickpocketed. She had noticed the missing wallet quickly and alerted the Officer within a couple of minutes. Four persons stated that they saw a couple suspiciously close to the woman when she was in line to greet one of the NYS officials. Because the exit door was under video surveillance, the Officer asked if anyone had seen anyone suspicious. Four witnesses all provided a statement to the Officer. The four persons described the two suspects with the following statements:

Witness 1: I saw a man and a woman who both looked intoxicated hovering close to the woman when she was waiting in line. They were both slender, around 130 pounds for the woman and 150 pounds for the guy. They both had dark hair and were wearing dark pants and black shoes. He was about 5'8" and she was about 5'8" in height.

Witness 2: The guy was about 6 feet tall and thin. Hard to tell because he was a little bent over, like he was drunk. He must have weighed no more than 160 pounds. She was thin, too. Around 120 pounds. They both had dark brown hair. She was probably about 5'6" tall. Her and the guy, they both had on black shoes. What got my attention at first was that they were both walking unevenly, like there was something wrong with them.

Witness 3: There was a man and a woman who were shaky and holding on to each other. The guy was about the same height as the woman, about 5'7". They were both skinny. They both had dark brown hair and black shoes. He must have weighed about 150 pounds, and she must have weighed around 130 pounds.

Witness 4: There was two of them that were near the woman. For some reason, I remember them. The man and the woman were both about 5'8" tall. They both had light hair and average build. He was probably around 190 pounds and she about 170 pounds. They seemed very quiet and weren't having any conversations.

Trooper Frank Perez is assigned to review the statements of the four witnesses. Based on the preceding information supplied by the four witnesses, Officer Perez should conclude that there is a problem with the description that was provided by witness number:

A. 1   C. 3
B. 2   D. 4

Answer 1

Answer question 1 based on the following "Miranda Warning."

Miranda Warning

"You have the right to remain silent when questioned.

Anything you say or do may be used against you in a court of law.

You have the right to consult an attorney before speaking to the police and to have an attorney present during questioning now or in the future.

If you cannot afford an attorney, one will be appointed for you before any questioning, if you wish.

If you decide to answer any questions now, without an attorney present, you will still have the right to stop answering at any time until you talk to an attorney.

Knowing and understanding your rights as I have explained them to you, are you willing to answer my questions without an attorney present?"

-----

1. According to the above version of the Miranda Warning, which of the following four actions by Trooper James Perkins is the most serious error?

A. Trooper Perkins asks the person being warned if he/she is willing to answer any questions without an attorney present after the person knows and understands his/her rights as explained.

(**CORRECT ACTION**. The last sentence states, "Knowing and understanding your rights as I have explained them to you, are you willing to answer my questions without an attorney present?" Statement "A" is therefore a correct statement and not the incorrect action that we are looking for.)

B. Trooper Perkings informs the person that anything the person says or does may be used against the person in a court of law.

(**CORRECT ACTION**. Sentence two states, "Anything you say or do may be used against you in a court of law." Statement "B" is therefore a correct action and not the incorrect statement that we are looking for.)

C. Trooper Perkins informs the person that if the person cannot afford an attorney, one will be appointed only at the time of trial.

(**INCORRECT ACTION**. **This is a serious error.** Therefore, "C" is the answer. Sentence four states, "If you cannot afford an attorney, one will be appointed for you <u>before any questioning</u>, if you wish.")

D. Trooper Perkins informs the person that a person without an attorney present has the right to stop answering at any time until the person talks to an attorney.

(**CORRECT ACTION**. Sentence five states, "If you decide to answer any questions now, without an attorney present, you will still have the right to stop answering at any time until you talk to an attorney." Statement "D" is therefore a correct action and not the incorrect statement that we are looking for.)

Answer Question 2 and 3 based on the following Penal Law S 240.40: Appearance in public under the influence of narcotics or a drug other than alcohol, and Criminal Procedure Law (CPL) S 160.10 When fingerprints may or must be taken

Penal Law (PL) S 240.40 Appearance in public under the influence of narcotics or a drug other than alcohol.

A person is guilty of appearance in public under the influence of narcotics or a drug other than alcohol when he appears in a public place under the influence of narcotics or a drug other than alcohol to the degree that he may endanger himself or other persons or property, or annoy persons in his vicinity. Appearance in public under the influence of narcotics or a drug other than alcohol is a violation.

Criminal Procedure Law (CPL) S 160.10 When fingerprints may or must be taken

Following an arrest, or following arraignment upon a local criminal court accusatory instrument, a defendant must be fingerprinted where the accusatory instrument charges:

(a) a felony

(b) a misdemeanor defined in the Penal Law

(c) a misdemeanor defined outside of the Penal Law which would constitute a felony if such person had a previous judgment of conviction for a crime

(d) loitering for the purposes of engaging in a prostitution offense (Penal Law 240.37)

After an arrest for any offense, fingerprints may be taken where:

(a) law enforcement is unable to ascertain the person's identity.

(b) identification given by such person may not be accurate.

(c) there is reasonable cause to believe the person might be sought by law enforcement officials for the commission of some other offense.

When fingerprints are required to be taken, photographs and palm prints may be taken.

-----

2. NYS State Trooper Marino arrests a person whom he reasonably believes is appearing in public under the influence of narcotics or a drug other than alcohol and who is annoying persons in his vicinity. The person provides acceptable I.D. (NYS issued driver's license with photo).

Which of the following actions by Trooper Marino is not an error?

A. Trooper Marino causes fingerprints to be taken because the person was arrested for an offense.

(WRONG. This is an error. Fingerprints must be taken when the arrest is for <u>specified</u> offenses ((a)-(d)) and not for just any offense.)

B. Trooper Marino causes photographs and palm prints to be taken because they must be taken whenever fingerprints are taken.

(WRONG. This is an error. CPL 160.10 states, "When fingerprints are required to be taken, photographs and palm prints <u>may</u> be taken" – the reverse meaning of answer B.)

C. Trooper Marino causes fingerprints to be taken because all drug offenses are felonies.

(WRONG. This is an error. All drug offenses are not felonies. One example is PL S 240, a violation.)

D. Trooper Marino prevents fingerprints to be taken because CPL S 160.10 does not authorize the taking of fingerprints in this particular instance.

(<u>CORRECT ACTION</u>. This is not an error. The offense is a violation, and not an offense specified in CPL 160.10 ((a)-(d)).

3.Trooper Janet Yaeger arrests a person for loitering for the purposes of engaging in a prostitution offense (Penal Law 240.37).

Which of the following actions by Trooper Yaeger is not an error?

A. She directs that fingerprints not be taken if the person is under the age of 18.

(WRONG. This is an error. CPL 160.10 does not specify any minimum age.)

B. She informs the officer taking fingerprints that fingerprints can only be taken if photographs and palm prints are also taken.

(WRONG. This is an error. CPL 160.10 states, "When fingerprints are required to be taken, photographs and palm prints <u>may</u> be taken" – the reverse meaning of answer B.)

C. She directs that fingerprints must be taken, even though Officer Yaeger personally knows the identity of the person arrested, who happens to be her next-door neighbor.

(CORRECT ACTION. This is not an error. CPL 160.10 states "Following an arrest, or following arraignment upon a local criminal court accusatory instrument, a defendant <u>must</u> be fingerprinted where the accusatory instrument charges...<u>loitering for purposes of engaging in a prostitution offense</u>....")

D. She informs the fingerprint officer that photographs and palm prints must be taken in all cases.

(WRONG. This is an error. CPL 160.10 states, "When fingerprints are required to be taken, photographs and palm prints <u>may</u> be taken.")

Answers 4-5

4. Trooper Sampson is the second Trooper to arrive at a suspected crime scene in a rest area building where a person is found dead on the floor. The first Trooper to arrive was Trooper Fuller. Trooper Sampson quickly reviews the actions taken by Trooper Fuller. Which of the following actions by Trooper Fuller is not in accordance with the above "Crime Scene General Procedure"?

A. Trooper Fuller documented the scene as per Procedure CSI-265(2017).

B. After Trooper Fuller received authorization as per form UARF-1867(2015), he withdrew security from the scene and allowed unrestricted access.

C. Trooper Fuller only allowed access to the scene by authorized persons and equipment.

D. Trooper Fuller did not review any of the actions taken by medical personnel that arrived on the scene, even if they interfered with evidence collection, because he did not want to get in the way of medical treatments.

(Procedure number 2 states, "If medical and other responders are on the scene, advise them of the requirement that evidence be preserved.")

----

5. Which of the following four choices in not in accordance with the above "Crime Scene General Procedure."?

A. Preserve all evidence and record the evidence, as per EDCI-337(2014).

B. Establish security and permit access or exit to only authorized persons and equipment.

C. Preserve all evidence and record the evidence, as per EDCI-337(2014).

D. Document the scene as per Procedure CSI-256(2017). (Correct number is <u>265</u>(2017).

Answer 6

During a city marathon, one of the participants was robbed by a spectator. Four runners stated that they witnessed the robbery. The four runners voluntarily described the suspects with the following statements.

Runner 1: There were two of them, one male and one female, both wearing light jackets. The guy was around 5'10" and the woman was about 5'6". He was muscular, but she looked very slender. Both were wearing blue jeans. His were dark and hers were light. They had on white sneakers and no glasses. He was probably around 190 pounds. She was probably around 125 pounds.

Runner 2: A man and a woman did the robbery. The guy was big and she was the skinny, shorter type. He was about 5'9". I think he had dark hair and she had dirty blonde hair. Both were wearing some type of thin jackets, the windbreaker type, and blue jeans. I would say he was about 170-180 pounds. She was probably around 120-140 pounds. I didn't notice the shoes.

Runner 3: The guy was medium size, like the woman. She had dark hair, not too long, and he had brown or black hair. They were both wearing sneakers, white, I think. They were about the same height, 5'6", and they were wearing khaki colored pants. I think they had sweaters on.

Runner 4: I didn't get a very good look at them, but one was a guy and one was a woman. He was about 5'9". She was about 5 inches shorter than him. He, 189, she 140 pounds. She was a blonde. I think he had dark brown hair. What I remember most is their thin jackets. I think both jackets had some type of logo on the front chest pocket. He was pretty muscular and she was slender.

Trooper Frank Perez is assigned to review the statements of the four witnesses. Based on the preceding information supplied by the four witnesses, Officer Perez should conclude that there is a problem with the description that was provided by witness number:

A. 1   C. 3
B. 2   D. 4

The answer for question number 6 is C. 3 (witness number 3). (The three other witnesses described the man as "muscular" and the woman as being "slender" or "skinny." Witness three described both as being of "medium size." Also, witness number three described the woman's hair as "dark," whereas the other three witnesses described the hair as "light", "dirty blonde," or just "blond." Finally, all the other witnesses described the pants of both suspects as "jeans," or "blue jeans," whereas witness number three described them as "khaki pants."

runner	suspects	gender	height	build	weight	hair	pants	jacket	shoes
1	2	M F	5'10" 5'6"	muscular slender	190 lbs 125 lbs	dark light	light jeans dark jeans	light	both white sneakers
2	2	M F	5'9" shorter	big skinny	170-180 lbs 120-140 lbs	dark, dirty blonde	blue jeans	thin	didn't notice shoes
3	2	M F	both 5'6"	**medium size**	----------	black **dark**	**khaki pants**	sweaters	both white sneakers
4	2	M F	5'9" 5'4"	muscular slender	180 lbs 140 lbs	dark brown, blonde	----------	thin	no mention

Answer 7

At an official NYS governmental function, a woman notified a NYS Officer that she had been pickpocketed. She had noticed the missing wallet quickly and alerted the Officer within a couple of minutes. Four persons stated that they saw a couple suspiciously close to the woman when she was in line to greet one of the NYS officials. Because the exit door was under video surveillance, the Officer asked if anyone had seen anyone suspicious. Four witnesses all provided a statement to the Officer. The four persons described the two suspects with the following statements:

witness	suspects	gender	height	build	weight	hair	pants	shoes	behavior
1	2	M F	5' 8" 5' 8"	slender slender	150 130	both dark	--------	black	both looked intoxicated
2	2	M F	6 feet 5' 6"	thin thin	160 120	both dark brown	both dark	black	they were both walking unevenly
3	2	M F	5'7" 5'7"	skinny skinny	150 130	both dark brown	both brown	black	they were shaky and holding on to each other
4	2	M F	5'8" 5'8"	**average build**	**190** **170**	**both light hair**	both dark	black	they didn't say anything

Witness 1: I saw a man and a woman who both looked intoxicated hovering close to the woman when she was waiting in line. They were both slender, around 130 pounds for the woman and 150 pounds for the guy. They both had dark hair and were wearing dark pants and black shoes. He was about 5'8" and she was about 5'8" in height.

Witness 2: The guy was about 6 feet tall and thin. Hard to tell because he was a little bent over, like he was drunk. He must have weighed no more than 160 pounds. She was thin, too. Around 120 pounds. They both had dark brown hair. She was probably about 5'6" tall. Her and the guy, they both had on black shoes. What got my attention at first was that they were both walking unevenly, like there was something wrong with them.

Witness 3: There was a man and a woman who were shaky and holding on to each other. The guy was about the same height as the woman, about 5'7". They were both skinny. They both had dark brown hair and black shoes. He must have weighed about 150 pounds, and she must have weighed around 130 pounds. Pants on both were brown.

Witness 4: There was two of them that were near the woman. For some reason, I remember them. The man and the woman were both about 5'8" tall. They both had light hair and average build. He was probably around 190 pounds and she about 170 pounds. They seemed very quiet and weren't having any conversations. Their shoes were black and their pants dark.

Trooper Frank Perez is assigned to review the statements of the four witnesses. Based on the preceding information supplied by the four witnesses, Officer Perez should conclude that there is a problem with the description that was provided by witness number:

A. 1   C. 3
B. 2   **D. 4**

The answer for question number 7 is <u>D. 4 (witness number 4).</u> (The three other witnesses described both the man and the woman as "slender" or "skinny." Witness 4 described them as being of "average build." Also, witness 4 described their hair as "light," whereas the other three described the hair of both persons as "brown" or "dark brown." Finally, witness 4 estimated the weights of the man and woman as 190 and 170 pounds, which is about 40 pound more than the weights estimated by the other three witnesses.

----

7. <u>DEDUCTIVE REASONING</u>

These questions evaluate your ability to apply regulations, procedures, or general rules to specific scenarios or to arrive at a conclusion from stated principles.

1. In one version of this type of question, a law definition or section of law is provided which you must apply to a given scenario.

2. Another version of this type of question asks you to categorize a specific case based on a classification scheme (verbal or numerical) that is provided.

3. Another version may test your ability to understand and follow rules or procedures.

Sometimes a question of this type may be difficult to answer, especially when the question involves a detailed procedure or complex section of law.
When answering a question of this type, try to understand fully the procedure or law. More than one reading may be necessary. As you read, try to see the relationships among the details provided.
Keep in mind that although it may be possible to answer very quickly some questions in other sections of the exam, the questions in this section may require more concentration and time.

Answer question 1 based on the information provided in the following summary of section of PL 120.60.

PL § 120.60 Stalking in the first degree

A person is guilty of stalking in the first degree when he or she commits the crime of stalking in the third degree as defined in subdivision three of section 120.50 or stalking in the second degree as defined in section 120.55 of this article and, in the course and furtherance thereof, he or she:

1. intentionally or recklessly causes physical injury to the victim of such crime, or

2. commits a class A misdemeanor defined in article one hundred thirty of this chapter, or a class E felony defined in section 130.25, 130.40 or 130.85 of this chapter, or a class D felony defined in section 130.30 or 130.45 of this chapter.

Stalking in the first degree is a class D felony.

-----

1. According to the preceding definition of stalking in the first degree, which of the following choices is an example of stalking in the first degree?

A. A male intentionally or recklessly causes physical injury to the victim of any crime.

B. A male or female commits a class A misdemeanor defined in article one hundred thirty of this chapter, or a class E felony defined in section 130.25, 130.40 or 130.85 of this chapter, or a class D felony defined in section 130.30 or 130.45 of this chapter (PL).

C. An adult intentionally or recklessly causes physical injury to the victim of a crime; or commits a class A misdemeanor defined in article one hundred thirty of this chapter, or a class E felony defined in section 130.25, 130.40 or 130.85 of this chapter, or a class D felony defined in section 130.30 or 130.45 of this chapter (PL).

D. none of the above

Answer question 2 based on the information provided in the following section of CPL 720.10.

CPL § 720.10 Youthful offender procedure; definition of terms

As used in this article, the following terms have the following meanings:

1. "Youth" means a person charged with a crime alleged to have been committed when he was at least 16 years old and less than 19 years old or a person charged with being a juvenile offender (ages 13, 14 or 15) as defined in subdivision forty-two of section 1.20 of this chapter.

2. "Eligible youth" means a youth who is eligible to be found a youthful offender. Every youth is so eligible unless:

(a) the conviction to be replaced by a youthful offender finding is for (i) a class A-I or class A-II felony, or (ii) an armed felony as defined in subdivision forty-one of section 1.20, except as provided in subdivision three, or (iii) rape in the first degree, criminal sexual act in the first degree, or aggravated sexual abuse, except as provided in subdivision three, or

(b) such youth has previously been convicted and sentenced for a felony, or

(c) such youth has previously been adjudicated a youthful offender following conviction of a felony or has been adjudicated on or after September first, nineteen hundred seventy-eight a juvenile delinquent who committed a designated felony act as defined in the family court act.

-----

2. According to the preceding, which one of the following persons qualifies as an "eligible youth"?

A. Bernard Cranson, male, 20 years old, is arrested and charged with a crime. He was never found to be a juvenile offender.

B. Martin Frieds, male, 20 years old, is arrested and charged with a crime. He has previously been adjudicated a youthful offender following conviction of a felony.

C. Cecilia Norwin, a female, 17 years old, is arrested and charged with a crime. She had previously been adjudicated a youthful offender following a conviction and sentencing for a felony.

D. none of the above

Answer 1

Answer question 1 based on the information provided in the following summary of section of PL 120.60.

PL § 120.60 Stalking in the first degree

A person is guilty of stalking in the first degree when he or she commits the crime of stalking in the third degree as defined in subdivision three of section 120.50 or stalking in the second degree as defined in section 120.55 of this article <u>and, in the course and furtherance thereof, he or she:</u>

1. intentionally or recklessly causes physical injury to the victim of such crime, or

2. commits a class A misdemeanor defined in article one hundred thirty of this chapter, or a class E felony defined in section 130.25, 130.40 or 130.85 of this chapter, or a class D felony defined in section 130.30 or 130.45 of this chapter.

Stalking in the first degree is a class D felony.

(A couple of careful readings of the preceding section of law can help us to summarize it as follows: A person is guilty of stalking in the first degree **IF** the person in the process of committing the crime of stalking in the second degree or stalking in the third degree **ALSO** does at least one of the following:

1. intentionally or recklessly causes physical injury to the victim of the second or third degree stalking, OR

2. commits one of the specific A misdemeanors or E felonies listed in PL 120.60.

Stalking in the first degree is a class D felony))

-----

1. According to the preceding definition of stalking in the first degree, which of the following choices is an example of stalking in the first degree?

A. A male intentionally or recklessly causes physical injury to the victim of any crime.

(WRONG. According to our summary, the physical injury must be in the course of committing stalking in the second degree or stalking in the third degree and other specified offense.)

B. A male or female commits a class A misdemeanor defined in article one hundred thirty of this chapter, or a class E felony defined in section 130.25, 130.40 or 130.85 of this chapter, or a class D felony defined in section 130.30 or 130.45 of this chapter (PL).

(WRONG. According to our summary, the offense must be in the course of committing stalking in the second degree or stalking in the third degree.)

C. An adult intentionally or recklessly causes physical injury to the victim of a crime; or commits a class A misdemeanor defined in article one hundred thirty of this chapter, or a class E felony defined in section 130.25, 130.40 or 130.85 of this chapter, or a class D felony defined in section 130.30 or 130.45 of this chapter (PL).

(WRONG. According to our summary, the physical injury must be in the course of committing stalking in the second degree or stalking in the third degree.)

D. none of the above

(THIS IS THE RIGHT CHOICE. All the other choices ("A", "B," and "C") do not consider that the physical injury or commission of any of the specified crimes <u>must</u> be during the commission of stalking in the second degree or stalking in the third degree.)

Answer 2

Answer question 2 based on the information provided in the following section of CPL 720.10.

CPL § 720.10 Youthful offender procedure; definition of terms

As used in this article, the following terms have the following meanings:

1. "Youth" means a person charged with a crime alleged to have been committed when he was at least 16 years old and less than 19 years old or a person charged with being a juvenile offender (ages 13, 14 or 15) as defined in subdivision forty-two of section 1.20 of this chapter.

2. "Eligible youth" means a youth who is eligible to be found a youthful offender. Every youth is so eligible unless:

(a) the conviction to be replaced by a youthful offender finding is for (i) a class A-I or class A-II felony, or (ii) an armed felony as defined in subdivision forty-one of section 1.20, except as provided in subdivision three, or (iii) rape in the first degree, criminal sexual act in the first degree, or aggravated sexual abuse, except as provided in subdivision three, or

(b) such youth has previously been convicted and sentenced for a felony, or

(c) such youth has previously been adjudicated a youthful offender following conviction of a felony or has been adjudicated on or after September first, nineteen hundred seventy-eight a juvenile delinquent who committed a designated felony act as defined in the family court act.

-----

2. According to the preceding, which one of the following persons qualifies as an "eligible youth"?

A. Bernard Cranson, male, 20 years old, is arrested and charged with a crime. He was never found to be a juvenile offender.

(DOES NOT QUALIFY. The youth has to be less than 19 years old (See "1" in section 720.10)

B. Martin Frieds, male, 20 years old, is arrested and charged with a crime. He has previously been adjudicated a youthful offender following conviction of a felony.

(DOES NOT QUALIFY. The youth has to be less than 19 years old (See "1" in section 720.10).

C. Cecilia Norwin, a female, 17 years old, is arrested and charged with a crime. She had previously been convicted and sentenced for a felony.

(DOES NOT QUALIFY. The section states, **"2.** Eligible youth means a youth who is eligible to be found a youthful offender. <u>Every youth is so eligible **unless**... (b) such youth has previously been adjudicated a youthful offender following a conviction and sentencing for a felony</u>." Ms. Norwin was previously convicted and sentenced for a felony.)

D. none of the above

(THIS IS THE ANSWER because none of the preceding three persons qualify as a youthful offender.)

Answer questions 3 - 4 based on the information provided in the following summaries of two Penal Law and Criminal Procedure Law sections.

Penal Law (PL) S 240.40 Appearance in public under the influence of narcotics or a drug other than alcohol.

A person is guilty of appearance in public under the influence of narcotics or a drug other than alcohol when he appears in a public place under the influence of narcotics or a drug other than alcohol to the degree that he may endanger himself or other persons or property, or annoy persons in his vicinity. Appearance in public under the influence of narcotics or a drug other than alcohol is a violation.

Criminal Procedure Law (CPL) S 160.10 When fingerprints may or must be taken

Following an arrest, or following arraignment upon a local criminal court accusatory instrument, a defendant must be fingerprinted where the accusatory instrument charges:

(a) a felony

(b) a misdemeanor defined in the Penal Law

(c) a misdemeanor defined outside of the Penal Law which would constitute a felony if such person had a previous judgment of conviction for a crime

(d) loitering for the purposes of engaging in a prostitution offense (Penal Law 240.37)

After an arrest for any offense, fingerprints may be taken where:

(a) law enforcement is unable to ascertain the person's identity.

(b) identification given by such person may not be accurate.

(c) there is reasonable cause to believe the person might be sought by law enforcement officials for the commission of some other offense.

When fingerprints are required to be taken, photographs and palm prints may be taken.

-----

3. Police Officer Marino arrests a person whom he reasonably believes is appearing in public under the influence of narcotics or a drug other than alcohol and who is annoying persons in his vicinity. The person provides acceptable I.D. (NYS issued driver's license with photo).

Which of the following choices is correct with respect to requiring fingerprints from the person arrested?

A. Fingerprints must be taken because the person was arrested for an offense.

B. Because fingerprints are required for any arrest as per PL S 240.0, photographs and palm prints may be taken.

C. Fingerprints must be taken because all drug offenses are felonies.

D. CPL S 160.10 does not authorize the taking of fingerprints in this particular instance.

----

4. Police Officer Janet Yaeger arrests a person for loitering for the purposes of engaging in a prostitution offense (Penal Law 240.37). Which of the following four statements is correct?

A. Fingerprints must be taken only if the person is of the age of 18 or over.

B. Fingerprints can only be taken if photographs and palm prints are also taken.

C. Fingerprints must be taken, even if Officer Yaeger personally knows the identity of the person arrested.

D. Photographs and palm prints must be taken.

Answer 3

3. Police Officer Marino arrests a person whom he reasonably believes is appearing in public under the influence of narcotics or a drug other than alcohol and who is annoying persons in his vicinity. The person provides acceptable I.D. (NYS issued driver's license with photo).

Which of the following choices is correct with respect to requiring fingerprints from the person arrested?

A. Fingerprints must be taken because the person was arrested for an offense.

(WRONG. Fingerprints must be taken when the arrest is for <u>specified</u> offenses ((a)-(d)) and not for just any offense.)

B. Because fingerprints are required for an arrest as per PL S 240.40, photographs and palm prints may be taken.

(WRONG. PL 240.40 is for a <u>violation</u> (and is not an offense listed in CPL 160.10 ((a)-(d))

C. Fingerprints must be taken because all drug offenses are felonies.

(WRONG. All drug offenses are not felonies. One example is PL S 240, a violation.)

D. CPL S 160.10 does not authorize the taking of fingerprints in this particular instance.

(CORRECT. The offense is a violation, and not an offense specified in CPL 160.10 ((a)-(d)).

Answer 4

4. Police Officer Janet Yaeger arrests a person for loitering for the purposes of engaging in a prostitution offense (Penal Law 240.37). Which of the following four statements is correct?

A. Fingerprints must be taken only if the person is of the age of 18 or over.

(WRONG. CPL 160.10 does not specify any minimum age.)

B. Fingerprints can only be taken if photographs and palm prints are also taken.

(WRONG. CPL 160.10 states, "When fingerprints are required to be taken, photographs and palm prints <u>may</u> be taken" – the reverse meaning of answer B.)

C. Fingerprints must be taken, even if Officer Yaeger personally knows the identity of the person arrested.

(CORRECT. CPL 160.10 states "Following an arrest, or following arraignment upon a local criminal court accusatory instrument, a defendant <u>must</u> be fingerprinted where the accusatory instrument charges...<u>loitering for purposes of engaging in a prostitution offense</u>....")

D. Photographs and palm prints must be taken.

(WRONG. CPL 160.10 states, "When fingerprints are required to be taken, photographs and palm prints <u>may</u> be taken.")

Questions 5-6

Use the following list of felony classes, the possible jail sentences, and examples of the types of offenses to answer questions 5 and 6.:

Felony Classes and Sentences

Offense / Sentence
'A' Violent Felony / Life, 20-25 years
(Arson in the first degree, crime of terrorism, murder in the first degree)

'B' Violent Felony / 5-25 years
Assault in the first degree, rape in the first degree, kidnapping in the second degree)

'B' Non Violent Felony / 1-3, Max 25 years
(Conspiracy in the second degree, bribery in the first degree, sex trafficking)

'C' Violent Felony / 3 1/2 to 15 years
(burglary in the second degree, gang assault in the second degree, aggravated manslaughter in the second degree)

'C' Non Violent Felony / No Jail, Probation, 1-2 years to 15 years
(arson in the third degree, computer tampering in the first degree, forgery in the first degree)

5. Officer Watson arrests an individual whom he processes at central booking and who is charged by the DA with the offense of sex trafficking. Based on the above "Felony Classes and Sentences," what is the longest term of imprisonment that the person can receive if he is found guilty?

A. 1-3 years
B. 20-25 years
C. 3 years
D. 25 years

----

6. Which of the following offenses has the least minimum sentence?
A. aggravated manslaughter in the second degree
B. burglary in the second degree
C. kidnapping in the second degree
D. forgery in the first degree (No jail)

Answer 5: D. 25 years

Answer 6. Which of the following offenses has the least minimum sentence?
A. aggravated manslaughter in the second degree (3 and 1/2 years)
B. burglary in the second degree (2 and 1/2 years)
C. kidnapping in the second degree (5 years)
D. forgery in the first degree (No jail)
Answer 6: D. forgery in the first degree (No jail)

---

8. INDUCTIVE REASONING

These questions test your ability to combine details or separate pieces of information to form general rules or a conclusion so that you may correctly answer a question based on a scenario that is provided.

The information provided may include sections of law, procedures, policies, or situations.

More than one careful reading of the information may be necessary before answering the question.

Question 1:   Time Limitations for the Commencement of a Criminal Action

Type of Offense	For the commencement of a criminal action to be timely, an accusatory instrument must be filed within the following time periods after the commission of the offense
Class "A" felony (or rape in the first degree (130.35 PL), or criminal sexual act in the first degree (130.50 PL), or aggravated sexual abuse in the first degree (130.70 PL) or sexual conduct against a child in the first degree	any time
any other felony	within 5 years
misdemeanor	within 2 years
petty offense	within 1 year

1. Based on the above table, which of the following statements is not correct?

A. Prosecution for any felony must be commenced within 5 years of commission of the offense.

B. Where the offense is a misdemeanor, for the commencement of a criminal action to be timely, an accusatory instrument must be filed within 2 years following the commission of the offense.

C. Where the offense charged is aggravated sexual abuse in first degree (130.70 PL), for the commencement of a criminal action to be timely, an accusatory instrument may be filed at any time following the commission of the offense.

D. Where the offense is a petty offense, for the commencement of a criminal action to be timely, an accusatory instrument must be filed within 1 year following the commission of the offense.

Answer 1

A. Prosecution for any felony must be commenced within 5 years of commission of the offense.

The statement is not correct because for certain felonies the prosecution can begin at any time after the offense is committed. These felonies are: "Class "A" felony (or rape in the first degree (130.35 PL), or criminal sexual act in the first degree (130.50 PL), or aggravated sexual abuse in the first degree (130.70 PL) or sexual conduct against a child in the first degree)."

Questions 2 - 3

Answer questions 2 - 3 based on the following summary of "CPL 100.10 Definitions of Local Criminal Court Accusatory Instruments."

CPL 100.10 Definitions of Local Criminal Court accusatory instruments

1. An **Information** is a verified written accusation by a person, charging person(s) with offense(s), none of which is a felony. It may serve as the basis for the commencement of an action and for prosecution.

2. A **Simplified information** is a written accusation by a police officer (or other public servant authorized to issue a simplified information).

> **1.** A **Simplified parks information** charges parks/recreation offense(s) less than a felony.

> **2.** A **Simplified environmental conservation information** charges environmental conservation offense(s) less than a felony.

> **3.** A **Simplified traffic information** charges traffic infractions or misdemeanors.

3. A **Prosecutor's information** is a written accusation filed by the DA, either at the direction of the grand jury or at the direction of the local criminal court, or at the DA's own instance, and charges offense(s) less than a felony.

4. A **Misdemeanor complaint** is a verified written accusation by a person charging offense(s), at least one of which is a misdemeanor, and none is a felony.

5. A **Felony complaint** is a verified written accusation by a person which charges offense(s), one or more of which must be felonies.

-----

2. Based on the preceding (CPL 100.10) definitions, which of the following statements is correct?

A. A Prosecutor's information is the same as a misdemeanor complaint.

B. A felony complaint must be filed by the D.A.

C. A Simplified Parks Information charges a felony.

D. A felony complaint charges at least one felony.

----

3. Police Officer Gonzalez is reviewing the above definitions sheet of Local Criminal Court accusatory instruments. Based on the definitions, he may correctly conclude that:

A. All accusatory instruments can charge any offense.

B. Simplified informations may be issued by all citizens.

C. Prosecutor's informations and misdemeanor complaints can charge misdemeanors and felonies.

D. None of the above.

Answers 2 - 3

2. Based on preceding (CPL 100.10) definitions, which of the following statements is correct?

A. A Prosecutor's information is the same as a misdemeanor complaint.

(WRONG. A Prosecutor's Information is a written accusation by the <u>D.A.</u>, whereas a misdemeanor complaint is a written accusation by <u>a person</u>.)

B. A felony complaint must be filed by the D.A.

(WRONG. A felony complaint is a written accusation by <u>a person</u>.)

C. A Simplified Parks Information charges a felony.

(WRONG. A Simplified Parks Information charges <u>less than a felony</u>.)

D. A felony complaint charges at least one felony.

(CORRECT. A felony complaint is a verified written accusation by a person which charges offense(s), <u>one or more of which must be felonies</u>.)

----

3. Police Officer Gonzalez is reviewing the above definitions sheet of Local Criminal Court accusatory instruments. Based on the definitions, he may correctly conclude that:

A. All accusatory instruments can charge any offense.

(WRONG. Accusatory instruments can charge only <u>specified</u> offenses.)

B. Simplified informations may be issued by all citizens.

(WRONG. Simplified informations can be issued only by a <u>police officer</u> or by other <u>authorized public servants</u>.)

C. Prosecutor's informations and misdemeanor complaints can charge misdemeanors and felonies.

(WRONG. Prosecutor's informations and misdemeanor complaints <u>cannot charge felonies</u>.)

D. None of the above.

(CORRECT ANSWER. All other choices are incorrect.)

Questions 4 - 5

4. While you are on patrol, a male, about 21 years old, reports that he had chained his bicycle to a bicycle parking station and gone into a drugstore to purchase shampoo, only to discover when he came out of the store that his bicycle chain had been cut and his bicycle stolen. You question four witnesses who give you four statements. Which of the following four statements is most likely to be incorrect?

A. The person who cut the chain and rode away with the bicycle was a male, white, about 21 years old and about six feet tall. He was wearing white sneakers, blue dungarees, a yellow T-shirt, and a dark brown backpack. He headed north for one block and then made a left turn.

B. The person who cut the chain was a male, white, about six feet tall. He was wearing black sneakers, blue dungarees, a yellow T-shirt, and a dark brown backpack. He rode the bicycle north for one block and then made a left turn.

C. The person who cut the chain and rode away with the bicycle was a male, white, about six feet tall. He was wearing black sneakers, blue dungarees, a yellow T-shirt, and a dark brown backpack. He pedaled north for one block and then made a left turn.

D. The person who cut the chain and rode away with the bicycle was a male, white, about six feet tall. He was wearing black sneakers, blue dungarees, a yellow T-shirt, and a dark brown backpack. He headed north for one block and then made a left turn.

----

5. Four witnesses to a hit and run accident tell Police Officer Tumi that they memorized the license plate of the car that sped away from the accident. Which of the following is the most like to be correct?

A. 9237SFG   C. 9537SFG

B. 9587SFG   D. 9531SFG

Answers 4 - 5

4. While you are on patrol, a male, about 21 years old, reports that he had chained his bicycle to a bicycle parking station and gone in to a drugstore to purchase shampoo, only to discover when he came out of the store that his bicycle chain had been cut and his bicycle stolen. You question four witnesses who give you four statements. Which of the following four statements is most likely to be incorrect?

A. The person who cut the chain and rode away with the bicycle was a male, white, about 21 years old and about six feet tall. He was wearing white sneakers, blue dungarees, a yellow T-shirt, and a dark brown backpack. He headed north for one block and then made a left turn.

(MOST LIKELY TO BE INCORRECT. Although the details of this statement agree with most of the other details in the other three statements below, this statement is the only one which describes the sneakers as being "white" instead of "black.")

B. The person who cut the chain was a male, white, about six feet tall. He was wearing black sneakers, blue dungarees, a yellow T-shirt, and a dark brown backpack. He rode the bicycle north for one block and then made a left turn.

C. The person who cut the chain and rode away with the bicycle was a male, white, about six feet tall. He was wearing black sneakers, blue dungarees, a yellow T-shirt, and a dark brown backpack. He pedaled north for one block and then made a left turn.

D. The person who cut the chain and rode away with the bicycle was a male, white, about six feet tall. He was wearing black sneakers, blue dungarees, a yellow T-shirt, and a dark brown backpack. He headed north for one block and then made a left turn.

----

5. Four witnesses to a hit and run accident tell Police Officer Tumi that they memorized the license plate of the car that sped away from the accident. Which of the following is the most likely to be correct?

A. 9237SFG (Choice "A" is not the most likely to be correct because the second numeral "2" differs from the "5" of the other three choices.)

B. 9587SFG (Choice "B" is also not the most likely to be correct because the third numeral "8" differs from the "3" of the other three choices.)

C. 9537SFG ((Choice "C" is the most likely to be correct. This is the plate number whose numerals agree with most other plate numbers.)

D. 9531SFG (Choice "D" is also <u>not</u> the most likely to be correct because the fourth numeral "1" differs from the "7" of the other three choices.)

Question 6

Answer question 6 based on the following table:

Summonses and Desk Appearance Tickets Issued by Police Officer Rinder

Week	Dates	Parking Summonses	Moving Summonses	Desk Appearance Tickets
1	June 1 – 7	24	11	4
2	June 8 - 14	21	8	7
3	June 15 – 21	26	12	2
4	June 22 – 28	19	9	6
5	June 29 – July 5	28	13	9

6. Police Officer Rinder is adding up the total number of summonses and desk appearance tickets issued by her during the above five-week period. Which of the following four formulas should she use to arrive at the correct total of summonses and desk appearance tickets that she issued?

A. 24+21+26+19+28

B. 28 + 13 + 9

C. 24+11+4+21+8+7+26+12+2+19+9+6+28+13+9

D. 1(24+11+4) + 2(21+8+7) + 3(26+12+2) + 4(19+9+6) + 5(28+13+9)

Answer 6

A. 24+21+26+19+28

(NOT CORRECT. This only includes "Parking Summonses" and does not include "Moving Summonses" and "Desk Appearance Tickets.")

B. 28 + 13 + 9

(NOT CORRECT. This only includes summonses and Desk Appearance Tickets issued during the fifth week, June 29 – July 5).

C. 24+11+4+21+8+7+26+12+2+19+9+6+28+13+9 (Total is 199.)

(CORRECT. This includes all the summonses and Desk Appearance Tickets issued during the entire five weeks.)

D. 1(24+11+4) + 2(21+8+7) + 3(26ı12+2) + 4(19+9+6) + 5(28+13+9)

(NOT CORRECT. This mathematical formula would give a result of 617.)

Question 7

Answer question 7 based on the following information:

During the month of July 2016 there were 9 burglaries reported in Police Officer Callion's precinct. In two of the burglaries, neighbors reported that at the approximate time of the burglaries they witnessed a male white, average height, shoulder length, dark hair, "with about a one inch scar on his left cheek." Both times the man was carrying a large brown carton out of the residence that had been burglarized. They also reported that at both times he had been wearing a blue T-shirt, dark blue, dirty dungarees, and white sneakers.

-----

7. During his patrol, Officer Callion stops four white males for questioning. He had recorded in his memo book the description given by the two witnesses. Which piece of information should Officer Callion consider the most important and pay careful attention to in identifying the suspected burglar?

A. the dark blue, dirty dungarees

B. the shoulder length, dark hair

C. the approximately one inch scar on his left cheek

D. the blue T-shirt

Question 8

Answer question 8 based on the following information:

Prior to the start of his patrol, Officer Kevin Johnson learns at the precinct that a female, about 65 years old, had been mugged one hour earlier by a person who the victim described as a "white young man, about twenty years old, with dark hair tied in a shoulder length ponytail, and with severe acne on his face." She also described him as wearing black pants, a yellow T-shirt, and black sneakers.

-----

8. During his patrol, Officer Johnson sees a group of six white males, about 20-25 years old, standing in front of Ernie's Bar. Officer Johnson stops his patrol car about twenty feet away to get a better look at the six males. Which of the following parts of the description provided by the victim is most important for Officer Johnson to consider in his attempt to identify the possible suspect?

A. the yellow T-shirt

B. the shoulder length pony tail

C. the black sneakers

D. the acne on the alleged mugger

Questions 9-10

Answer questions 9 -10 based on the following information:

Police Officer Gravitz is assigned to patrol an area which includes four Housing Developments. During the prior four weeks, crime statistics show that four burglaries were reported at the Bellman Housing Development, all between the hours of 10:00 a.m. and 4:00 p.m. At the Diamond Housing Development ten robberies were reported. At the Adrian Housing Development seven mailboxes were broken into. At the Garnacy Housing Development four bicycles were stolen. The robberies all occurred between 9:30 a.m. and 4:30 p.m. The mailboxes were broken into between 9:30 a.m. and 10:30 a.m. The bicycles were all reported stolen in the afternoon and before 5:00 p.m.

-----

9. Officer Gravitz works the 9:00 a.m. to 5:00 p.m. tour. On Monday, his sergeant instructs him to pay careful attention to robberies. To try to reduce the number of robberies, Office Gravitz should patrol the:

A. Garnacy Housing Development

B. Bellman Housing Development

C. Adrian Housing Development

D. Diamond Housing Development

----

10. On Tuesday Officer Gravitz also works the 9:00 a.m. to 5:00 p.m. tour. On Tuesday, his sergeant tells him that three more mailboxes have been broken into at the same housing development that reported the prior break-ins and instructs him to pay careful attention to mailbox break-ins. To try to reduce the number of break-ins of mailboxes, Office Gravitz should patrol the:

A. Garnacy Housing Development

B. Bellman Housing Development

C. Adrian Housing Development

D. Diamond Housing Development

Answers 7-10

Answer question 7 based on the following information:

During the month of July 2016 there were 9 burglaries reported in Police Officer Callion's precinct. In two of the burglaries, neighbors reported that at the approximate time of the burglaries they witnessed a male white, average height, shoulder length, dark hair, "with about a one inch scar on his left cheek." Both times the man was carrying a large brown carton out of the residence that had been burglarized. They also reported that at both times he had been wearing a blue T-shirt, dark blue, dirty dungarees, and white sneakers.

-----

7. During his patrol, Officer Callion stops four white males for questioning. He had recorded in his memo book the description given by the two witnesses. Which piece of information should Officer Callion consider the most important and pay careful attention to in identifying the suspected burglar?

A. the dark blue, dirty dungarees (**WRONG.** A suspect can easily change dungarees. Also, many men wear blue, and sometimes dirty, dungarees.)

B. the shoulder length, dark hair (**WRONG.** Although the length of the hair may be useful, a suspect can easily change the length of the hair or the hair style.)

C. the approximately one inch scar on his left cheek (**CORRECT.** This is the best answer because a scar cannot easily be changed or hidden.)

D. the blue T-shirt (**WRONG.** A suspect can easily change his T-shirt. Also, blue T-shirts are common.)

Answer question 8 based on the following information:

Prior to the start of his patrol, Officer Kevin Johnson learns at the precinct that a female, about 65 years old, had been mugged one hour earlier by a person who the victim described as a "white young man, about twenty years old, with dark hair tied in a shoulder length ponytail, and with severe acne on his face." She also described him as wearing black pants, a yellow T-shirt, and black sneakers.

8. During his patrol, Officer Johnson sees a group of six white males, about 20-25 years old, standing in front of Ernie's Bar. Officer Johnson stops his patrol car about twenty feet away to get a better look at the six males. Which of the following parts of the description provided by the victim is most important for Officer Johnson to consider in his attempt to identify the possible suspect?

A. the yellow T-shirt **(WRONG.** A suspect can easily change his T-shirt.)

B. the shoulder length pony tail **(WRONG.** Although the length of the hair may be useful, a suspect can easily change the length of the hair or the hair style.)

C. the black sneakers **(WRONG.** A suspect can easily change his sneakers. Also, many men wear black sneakers.)

D. the acne on the alleged mugger (CORRECT. This is the best answer because acne cannot easily be changed or hidden.)

Answer questions 9 - 10 based on the following information:

Police Officer Gravitz is assigned to patrol an area which includes four Housing Developments. During the prior four weeks, crime statistics show that four burglaries were reported at the Bellman Housing Development, all between the hours of 10:00 a.m. and 4:00 p.m. At the Diamond Housing Development ten robberies were reported. At the Adrian Housing Development seven mailboxes were broken into. At the Garnacy Housing Development four bicycles were stolen. The robberies all occurred between 9:30 a.m. and 4:30 p.m. The mailboxes were broken into between 9:30 a.m. and 10:30 a.m. The bicycles were all reported stolen in the afternoon and before 5:00 p.m.

-----

9. Officer Gravitz works the 9:00 a.m. to 5:00 p.m. tour. On Monday, his sergeant instructs him to pay careful attention to robberies. To try to reduce the number of robberies, Office Gravitz should patrol the:

A. Garnacy Housing Development **(WRONG.** At the Garnacy Housing Development four bicycles were stolen.)

B. Bellman Housing Development **(WRONG** ... four burglaries were reported at the Bellman Housing Development....)

C. Adrian Housing Development **(WRONG.** At the Adrian Housing Development seven mailboxes were broken into.)

D. Diamond Housing Development (CORRECT. "At the Diamond Housing Development ten robberies were reported." He should patrol this development because it is the most likely housing development to have robberies.)

----

10. On Tuesday Officer Gravitz also works the 9:00 a.m. to 5:00 p.m. tour. On Tuesday, his sergeant tells him that three more mailboxes have been broken into at the same housing development that reported the prior break-ins and instructs him to pay careful attention to mailbox break-ins. To try to reduce the number of break-ins of mailboxes, Office Gravitz should patrol the:

A. Garnacy Housing Development **(WRONG. "**At the Garnacy Housing Development four <u>bicycles</u> were stolen.")

B. Bellman Housing Development **(WRONG. "**... four <u>burglaries</u> were reported at the Bellman Housing Development....")

C. Adrian Housing Development (CORRECT. During the prior four weeks, "At the Adrian Housing Development seven <u>mailboxes</u> were broken into.")

D. Diamond Housing Development **(WRONG. "**At the Diamond Housing Development ten <u>robberies</u> were reported.")

---

9. INFORMATION ORDERING

These questions evaluate your ability to put in order given rules or actions. The rules or actions can include letters, words, sentences, procedures, pictures, and logical or mathematical operations.

The key to answering this type of question correctly is to make sure that the directions are clear to you.

To obtain maximum clarity, take the time to understand the logical order of the directions. Steps that must be done "before" or "after" or "at the same time" should be noted.

Also, at the time of selecting your answer, refer back to the directions to make sure that you have not mentally mixed up the order or the details of the directions.

Question 1

Answer question 1 based on the following "Bomb Threat Procedure."

Bomb Threat Procedure

Some bomb threats are received by phone. A Police Officer who receives a bomb threat by phone should do the following in the order specified:

   1. Stay calm. Do not hang up, even if the caller hangs up. Be polite and show interest in what the caller is saying.

   2. If possible, write a message to a fellow officer or other NYC Police Department employee.

   3. If your phone displays the caller number, write down the number.

   4. Even if the caller hangs up, do not hang up your phone. Use a different phone that is not a cell phone to contact the "Bomb Threat Notification Unit."

   5. As soon as possible, complete the "Bomb Threat Checklist."

-----

1. At a "Bomb Threat Exercise" conducted at the precinct, you are told that you have answered a phone call during which a bomb threat is made. You have written a note and notified a Police Officer working at the desk next to yours. You have also written down the caller's number which displayed on your phone unit. The caller hangs up. The next step you should take is to:

A. Hang up the phone and immediately call the "Bomb Threat Notification Unit."

B. Do not hang up the phone, but use a cell phone to contact the "Bomb Threat Notification Unit."

C. Complete the form "Bomb Threat Checklist."

D. Do not hang up and use a different phone (not a cell phone) to contact the "Bomb Threat Notification Unit."

Answer 1

Answer question 1 based on the following "Bomb Threat Procedure."

1. At a "Bomb Threat Exercise" conducted at the precinct, you are told that you have answered a phone call during which a bomb threat is made. You have written a note and notified a Police Officer working at the desk next to yours. You have also written down the caller's number which displayed on your phone unit. The caller hangs up. The next step you should take is to:

A. Hang up the phone and immediately call the "Bomb Threat Notification Unit."

(WRONG. Number 1 states, "Do not hang up...")

B. Do not hang up the phone, but use a cell phone to contact the "Bomb Threat Notification Unit."

(WRONG. Number 3 states, "Use a different phone that is not a cell phone...")

C. Complete the form "Bomb Threat Checklist."

(WRONG. Number 5 states, "complete the form "Bomb Threat Checklist." This is the last step and is done after contacting the "Bomb Threat Notification Unit.")

D. Do not hang up and use a different phone (not a cell phone) to contact the "Bomb Threat Notification Unit."

(CORRECT. This is step number four and comes directly after step number three, "...write down the number," which you have already done.)

Question 2

Answer question 2 based on the following "Abandoned Vehicle Procedure."

Police Officer Palenco receives the following new "Abandoned Vehicle Procedure."

Abandoned Vehicle Procedure

1. An abandoned vehicle must be reported to Police Dispatch at 718-555-0105.

2. A police officer will be assigned to attach a notice on the vehicle instructing the owner to remove the vehicle within 48 hours.

3. If the vehicle is not removed within 72 hours, the same officer who reported the abandoned vehicle will complete an AVR (Abandoned Vehicle Information) form and submit it to the precinct (VR Office).

4. The VR office will assign the report an incident report number and e-mail it to the city Department of Environmental Hazards.

5. If the vehicle is not removed within 48 hours, the Department of Environmental Hazards will tow the vehicle to the Waste Metal Recovery Site located in the borough.

-----

2. Officer Palenco is informed by an angry shop owner that a vehicle has been parked in front of his store for the past 3 months without it ever being moved and has accumulated 22 parking tickets. According to the Abandoned Vehicle Procedure, Officer Polanco should:

A. Complete an AVR report and submit it to the precinct (VR Office), as three months have already passed and the shop owner is angry.

B. He should attach a notice on the vehicle instructing the owner to remove the vehicle within 48 hours.

C. Report the abandoned vehicle to Police Dispatch by informing his sergeant, as this will speed up the process.

D. Report the abandoned vehicle to Police Dispatch at 718-555-0105.

Answer 2

2. Officer Palenco is informed by an angry shop owner that a vehicle has been parked in front of his store for the past 3 months without it ever being moved and has accumulated 22 parking tickets. According to the Abandoned Vehicle Procedure, Officer Palenco should:

A. Complete an AVR report and submit it to the precinct (VR Office), as three months have already passed and the shop owner is angry.

(WRONG: The first thing he must do is report the abandoned vehicle to Police Dispatch at 718-555-0105.)

B. He should attach a notice on the vehicle instructing the owner to remove the vehicle within 48 hours.

(WRONG. <u>After</u> Police Officer Palenco reports the abandoned vehicle, "A police officer will be assigned to attach a notice on the vehicle instructing the owner to remove the vehicle within 48 hours.")

C. Report the abandoned vehicle to Police Dispatch by informing his sergeant, as this will speed up the process.

(WRONG. The report must be done by telephone and not to his sergeant. There are no steps in the procedure to "speed up the process.")

D. Report the abandoned vehicle to Police Dispatch at 718-555-0105.

(CORRECT. Regardless of how long the vehicle has been there or how angry the shop owner is, the correct first step is to report the abandoned vehicle to Police Dispatch.)

Question 3

Your supervisor gives you five "Complaint Forms" with the following priority numbers:

2867   19643   0344   783   8249

He asks you to organize the forms in ascending priority.

3. According to the above, the third Complaint Form would be Complaint Form number:

A. 8249   C. 783

B. 2867   D. 0344

Answer 3

Examples of <u>ascending order</u> and <u>descending order</u>

Ascending Priority Number Order	Descending Priority Number Order
1	5
2	4
3	3
4	2
5	1

The Complaint Forms in Ascending Priority Number Order are as follows:

1) 0344

2) 783

3) 2867

4) 8249

5) 19643

The third complaint number on the list is 2867, therefore the correct answer is **B) 2867**.

Question 4

Your supervisor gives you five "Requests for Investigation" forms submitted by residents in your precinct. The forms were submitted by the following five persons:

George Felder, Harriet Volker, Ben Halston, Abe Johnson, Diane Molton

He asks you to organize the forms in last name alphabetical order.

-----

4. According to the above, the fourth "Request for Investigation" form is the one submitted by:

A. Halston, Ben

B. Volker, Harriet

C. Molton, Diane

D. Felder, George

Answer 4

The correct listing in last name alphabetical order is:

1) Felder, George

2) Halston, Ben

3) Johnson, Abe

4) Molton, Diane

5) Volker, Harriet

The fourth name on the list is Molton, Diane, therefore the correct answer is **C) Molton, Diane**.

Question 5

5. The ninth letter of the alphabet is:

A) H   C) I

B) J   D. G

Answer 5

The letters of the alphabet (in order) are as follows:

A,   B,   C,   D,   E,   F,   G,   H,   I   J,   K,   L   M.....

1........2........3.........4........5.........6.........7........8.........9.........10.......11.......12.......13....

The correct answer is **C) I.**

Question 6

6. You are assigned to drive the precinct van. Your sergeant asks you to make five stops to pick up police officers. At the first two stops you are to pick up six police officers at each stop. At the last three stops you are to pick up four police officers at each stop. Which of the following mathematical expressions correctly states the total number of police officers that you will pick up at the five stops?

A) 2 + 6 + 3 + 4   B) 2 X 6 X 3 X 4   C) 2 + 3   D) 2(6) + 3(4)

Answer 6

At the first two stops you will pick up six police officers at each stop (6 + 6 = 12 police officers). At the last three stops you will pick up 4 police officers at each stop (4 + 4 + 4 = 12 police officers). The total number of police officers to be picked up is therefore 24 (because 12 + 12 = 24 police officers).

The A, B, C, and D choices would yield the following results:

A) 2 + 6 + 3 + 4 (This gives a total of 15).

B) 2 X 6 X 3 X 4 (This gives a total of 144.)

C) 2 + 3 (This gives a total of 5.)

D) 2(6) + 3(4) = 24 ((The mathematical expression 2(6) + 3(4) means (2 X 6) + (3 X 4) = 24. The correct answer therefore is **D) 2(6) + 3(4)**.)

Question 7

Organize the following four sentences in the best logical order:

1. This training includes classroom and "on the street" practice driving.

2. Because of this, they receive proper driving and safety instruction.

3. "On the street" driving is stressed and comprises eighty percent of the training time.

4. Police Officers may be assigned to drive a precinct van.

(A) 1, 3, 4, 2   (B) 2, 3, 4, 1   (C) 3, 2, 1, 4   (D) 4, 2, 1, 3

Answer 7

The correct answer is **(D) 4, 2, 1, 3.**

4. Police Officers may be assigned to drive a precinct van. (This sentence introduces the topic of driving a precinct van.)

2. Because of this, they receive proper driving and safety instruction.

1. This training includes classroom and "on the street" practice driving.

3. "On the street" driving is stressed and comprises eighty percent of the training time.

(After sentence 4, sentences 2, 1, and 3 follow logically in that order.)

Question 8

Your sergeant hands you five "Overtime Request Forms" which you submitted for processing. He reminds you that all overtime requests must be submitted in date order and numbered sequentially. The dates on the overtime forms are as follows:

10-4-2016   9/24/2016   October 1, 2016   September 28, 2016   Sept. 12, 2016

He asks you to number the forms in ascending date order and that you resubmit them.

Assuming that you organize the forms as your supervisor asks and that you number the first request "Request 1," which of the above dated requests would be numbered "Request 3"?

A. 10-4-2016   C. October 1, 2016

B. 9/24/2016   D. September 28, 2016

Answer 8

The correct ascending date order is:

         1) Sept. 12, 2016

         2) 9/24/2016

         3) September 28, 2016

         4) October 1, 2016

         5) 10-4-2016

The third date on the list is September 28, 2016. Therefore, the correct answer is

D). September 28, 2016.

Question 9

The following are four sentences. Each sentence (listed in random order) is one of the four steps necessary to attach a metal shield to the front of a van. Which one of the following choices (A, B, C, D) lists the order of sentences which best expresses the logical sequence of metal shield installation?

   1. Drive the van slowly forward to test whether the shield is securely bolted to the van.

2. Tighten the bolts with heavy duty nuts.

3. Align the front of the van with the shield connectors.

4. Insert connecting bolts in aligned holes of shield and the van's shield connectors.

A. 1, 4, 2, 3

B. 2, 3, 4, 1

C. 4, 1, 3, 2

D. 3, 4, 2, 1

Answer 9

The correct answer is **D. 3, 4, 2, 1.** (In this order, the sentences are logically connected.)

3. Align the front of the van with the shield connectors.

4. Insert connecting bolts in aligned holes of shield and the van's shield connector.

2. Tighten the bolts with heavy duty nuts.

1. Drive the van slowly forward to test whether the shield is securely bolted to the van.

----

10. PRACTICE TEST QUESTIONS

Answer questions 1 - 5 based on the information contained in the following paragraphs.

Police Officers Frank Torres and Diane Washington were on patrol on August 13, 2016 when at 9:45 p.m. they witnessed a minor traffic accident (at East 16th Street and Kings Highway in Brooklyn). Officer Torres called the Police Dispatcher at 9:50 p.m. and reported that the two drivers, and two passengers (one in each vehicle) did not sustain any personal injuries. One of the vehicles, the one driven by a male named Felix Upton, did have minor damage to the windshield, and the other vehicle, driven by a male named Mark Levington, had extensive damage to the driver's side front door.

Officer Washington examined the driver's licenses, vehicle registration certificates and vehicle insurance identification cards. The auto driven by Felix Upton, age 46, was a black 2012 Ford Edge, N.Y. license plate 4357ZB, owned by the driver, residing at 1942 West 58th Street, New York, N.Y. Mr. Upton's N.Y. driver's license identification number is D274 43 662 and the expiration date is December 31, 2016.

The driver of the other auto was Mark Levington, age 52, residing at 2686 Manor Street, Brooklyn, N.Y. Mr. Levington's auto was a blue 2011 Ford Escape, NY license plate 607PHB. Mr. Levington's driver's license identification number is A214 295 337 and the expiration is December 31, 2016.

Officers Torres and Washington completed a Vehicle Accident Report at 10:15 p.m. The report number was 48392747332.

-----

1. What is the time of the accident?

A. 9:50 p.m.

B. 10:15 p.m.

C. 9:45 p.m.

D. before 9:30 a.m.

----

2. How many persons were injured as a result of the traffic accident?

A. 1   C. 2

B. 0   D. none of the above

----

3. Which car sustained extensive damage to the driver's side front door?

A.   NY plate #607PHB, black 2012 Ford Edge

B.   NY plate #4357ZN, black 2012 Ford Edge

C.   NY plate #4357ZN, blue 2011 Ford Escape

D.   NY plate #607PHB, blue 2011 Ford Escape

----

4. Which of the following statements is not correct?

A. The auto driven by Felix Upton, age 46, was a black 2012 Ford Edge.

B. The vehicle Accident Report number was 4839274732.

C. Mark Levington, age 52, resides at 2686 Manor Street, Brooklyn, N.Y.

D. Mr. Upton's N.Y. driver's license identification number is D274 43 662.

----

5. Which of the following is correct?

A. The person residing at 1942 West 58th Street, New York, N.Y. has a N.Y. driver's license identification number D274 43 665 with an expiration date of December 31, 2016.

B. Mark Levington, age 25, resides at 2686 Manor Street, Brooklyn, N.Y.

C. The auto driven by Felix Upton, is a black 2012 Ford Edge, N.Y. license plate 4357ZB.

D. The accident occurred at East 16th Street and Kings Highway in the Bronx.

Answer questions 6 - 8 based on the following extracts of two Criminal Procedure Law sections, CPL 120.70 and CPL 120.80.

CPL 120.70 A warrant of arrest issued by a district court, NYC criminal court or a superior court judge sitting as a local criminal court can be executed anywhere in the state.

A warrant of arrest issued by a city, town, or village court can be executed in the county of issuance or adjoining county (or anywhere in NYS upon the written endorsement of a local criminal court of the county in which arrest is to be made).

CPL 120.80 A warrant of arrest is executed any day of the week, any hour of the day or night.

The arresting police officer is not required to have the warrant in his possession at the time of making the arrest.

-----

6. Police Officer Marino, a NYPD Officer assigned to a precinct in Queens County, has in his possession a warrant of arrest issued by a district court for a person named Jack Wringer. Which of the following choices is correct?

A. Police Officer Marino cannot execute the warrant of arrest because it was issued by a district court and not a New York City court.

B. Jack Wringer cannot be arrested on that warrant if he is outside the county served by the district court.

C. Police Officer Marino may execute the warrant outside the state of New York.

D. Police Officer Marino may execute the warrant because it was issued by a district court.

----

7. Police Officer Jane Goodwin, a NYPD Officer assigned to a precinct in Brooklyn, has in her possession a warrant of arrest issued by a town court in Nassau County. Which of the following statements is correct?

A. Officer Goodwin can execute the warrant in Brooklyn.

B. Officer Goodwin can execute the warrant only on weekdays in Brooklyn.

C. Officer Goodwin can execute the warrant in Brooklyn only if it has the written endorsement of a local criminal court of the county in which the arrest is to be made, in this case Kings County (Brooklyn).

D. Officer Goodwin can execute the warrant in New Jersey.

----

8. According to CPL 120.70, which of the following is not correct?

A. A warrant of arrest issued by a superior court judge sitting as a local criminal court can be executed anywhere in the state.

B. A warrant of arrest issued by the NYC criminal court can be executed anywhere in the state.

C. A warrant of arrest issued by the board of a school district can be executed anywhere in the state.

D. Some warrants of arrest may be executed anywhere in the state.

Question 9

At a civics day parade, a young woman approaches Officer Kevin Norville at the corner of Jefferson Avenue and 65th Street and quickly informs him that a few minutes earlier she had overheard two men in their late twenties discussing detonating bombs during the parade. They each had a bulky backpack on their shoulders. One of the men had black hair and a black backpack with a United States logo sewn on it. The other man had a grey backpack with a peace symbol sewn on it. This man had blonde hair. She didn't notice any other features because it all happened very quickly and she was in shock and very afraid to do or say anything. When she last saw them, they were walking on Jefferson Avenue toward 66th Street.

Officer Norville wishes to immediately transmit this information to the police control van several blocks away. Which of the following four versions of Officer Norvilles's proposed message is the best?

9. A. Send backup to the corner of Jefferson and 66th Street. Received a report that there are two bombers with backpacks in the vicinity. One has a black backpack and the other has a grey backpack with logos on them. Suggest you stop anyone with a backpack.

B. "Possible bomber situation. Several minutes ago, two men in their 20's were overheard planning to detonate bombs during the parade. Suspect number one has black hair and is shouldering a black backpack with a united states flag logo. Suspect number two has blonde hair and a grey backpack with a peace symbol logo. Last seen several minutes ago, walking on Jefferson toward 66."

C. Bomber situation. Two men were overheard planning to detonate bombs during the parade. Suspect number one has black hair and is shouldering a black backpack with a united states flag logo. Suspect number two has black hair and a grey backpack with a peace symbol logo. Last seen walking on Jefferson toward 66."

D. "Bomb alert. Two men wearing backpacks who were talking about exploding them. They are heading toward 66th Street. Suggest you stop and frisk them. The report is from a young woman."

----

10. The following question is comprised of a series of sentences which are in scrambled order. Select the order of sentences (A, B, C, or D) which most correctly and logically places the sentences in a meaningful and effective order.

1. Everyone is different, and there may be as many ways to study as there are people.
2. This does not mean, however, that all neural connections and all brains work alike.
3. Short sessions help the brain retain more, while studying over a period of time help to reinforce the neural connections in the brain.
4. Short study sessions over a long period of time are very helpful.
5. The manner and length of time that one practices answering questions can greatly affect the mark that one receives on an exam.

(A) 5-1-3-4-2
(B) 5-4-1-3-2

(C) 4-5-1-4-2
(D) 5-4-3-2-1

----

11. The following question is comprised of a series of sentences which are in scrambled order. Select the order of sentences (A, B, C, or D) which most correctly and logically places the sentences in a meaningful and effective order.

1. They are restricted to these two outward aims because to test legal expertise would be unfair to the general public.
2. This aim is probably the most important and merit worthy aspect of civil service exams.
3. A third, invisible aim, is fairness.
4. They are designed to test general knowledge and aptitude only.
5. Some competitive civil service exams for positions in the court system do not include legal definitions.

(A) 3-1-5-4-2
(B) 5-4-1-3-2

(C) 4-5-1-4-2
(D) 5-1-3-4-2

Answer questions 12 – 13 based on the following accident details.

Officer Nordstrum collects the following information at the scene of an auto accident:

Date of Accident: September 9, 2016

Time of accident: 4:15 p.m.

Place of accident: Intersection of Lavin Avenue and Reiker Avenue, Bronx

Driver: Barry Jones

Vehicle: 2008 Toyota Sienna

Damage: Vehicle struck a commercial metal garbage container protruding into the street.

-----

12. Officer Nordstrum is preparing a report of the accident and has four drafts of the report. He wishes to use the draft that expresses the information most clearly, accurately and completely. Which draft should he choose?

A. At 4:15 p.m., on September 9, 2016, at the intersection of Lavin Avenue and Reiker Avenue, Bronx, a vehicle driven by Barry Jones struck a commercial metal garbage container protruding into the street.

B. On September 9, 2016, at 4:15 p.m., at the intersection of Lavin Avenue and Reiker Avenue, Bronx, a 2008 Toyota Sienna driven by Barry Lones struck a commercial metal garbage container protruding into the street.

C. On September 9, 2016, at 4:25 p.m., at the intersection of Lavin Avenue and Reiker Avenue, Bronx, a 2008 Toyota Sienna driven by Barry Jones struck a commercial metal garbage container protruding into the street.

D. On September 9, 2016, at 4:15 p.m., at the intersection of Lavin Avenue and Reiker Avenue, Bronx, a 2008 Toyota Sienna driven by Barry Jones struck a commercial metal garbage container protruding into the street.

----

13. Officer Nordstrum is comparing the information he recorded in his memo pad (at the scene of the accident) to the information in his report. Which of the above choices (A, B, C, or D) has a detail that does not agree with the information in the officer's memo pad?

A. Date of Accident: September 9, 2016; Time of accident: 4:15 p.m.

B. Place of accident: Intersection of Lavin Avenue and Reiker Avenue, Bronx

C. Driver: Barry Jones: Vehicle: 2008 Toyota Sienna

D. Damage: Vehicle struck a commercial plastic garbage container protruding into the street

----

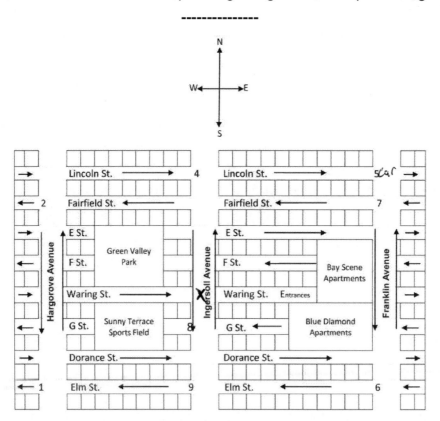

14. Your partner is driving south in your squad patrol car and the squad car is at the intersection of Lincoln St. and Franklin Avenue. You are informed that an auto accident has just occurred at the intersection of Waring Street and Ingersoll Avenue. Assuming you must

obey all traffic signs, which one of the following four choices describes the best statement you can give your partner as to the most direct route?

A. Drive south on Franklin Avenue to Fairfield St, then drive east on Fairfield St. to Ingersoll Avenue, then south to the intersection of Dorance Street and Ingersoll Avenue.

B. Drive south on Franklin Avenue to Fairfield St, then drive west on Fairfield St. to Ingersoll Avenue, then north to the intersection of Dorance Street and Ingersoll Avenue.

C. Drive north on Franklin Avenue to Fairfield St, then drive east on Fairfield St. to Ingersoll Avenue, then north to the intersection of Dorance Street and Ingersoll Avenue.

D. Drive south on Franklin Avenue to Fairfield St, then drive west on Fairfield St. to Ingersoll Avenue, then south to the intersection of Waring Street and Ingersoll Avenue.

----

15. Officer Faulk is asked by his sergeant to brief the new officers on the importance and proper use of incident reports, especially when each type of incident report is to be used. Officer Faulk knows that properly preparing reports is an important part of an officer's duties. This is especially true when filling out incident reports for "aided" cases or "unusual occurrences." An "Aided" report is used when an officer assists a state employee or member of the public who has been injured and required emergency or medical assistance. "Unusual Occurrence" reports are prepared for other types of incidents, including arrests and bomb threats. In addition to providing a paper trail for legal and liability reasons, these reports are a valuable resource when reviewing staffing, procedures, work performance, and court planning. Officer Faulk wishes to emphasize to the new officers what his sergeant suggested that he emphasize. Which of the following statements best reflects the wishes of the sergeant?

A. Please remember that an "Aided" incident report is used to document bomb threats.
B. Keep in mind that "Aided" and "Unusual Occurrence" reports prevent law suits against Court Officers.
C. Please remember that an "Aided" report is filled out if an officer calls for an ambulance for an injured person. An Unusual Incident Report is filled out for non-medical incidents.
D. Please keep in mind that an "Aided" report, and not an unusual incident report, must be filled out if a person with disabilities is a party in an active case.

----

16. Officer Holmes is giving a speech to the officers who have just been assigned to the magnetometer post that he supervises. He wishes to convey the following to the officers: Staffing a magnetometer post requires a number of skills. Among these skills is the ability to interact with the public and court employees in a firm, yet pleasant manner. Tact and patience on the part of Court Officers are often needed. In addition to developing and applying these two traits, Court Officers should also insure that they obtain sufficient daily sleep. This will help them feel more alert and less tired and anxious. It is also a good practice to take at least a ten-minute break after every hour of magnetometer duty. This will give both the body and mind the opportunity to "unwind" and recharge with fresh energy and attitude.

According to the preceding passage, which of the following possible statements by Officer Holmes best summarizes what Officer Holmes is trying to convey?
A. You are here because all officers should be trained in magnetometer operation.
B. Officers should get at least 8 hours of sleep each night.
C. Staffing a magnetometer post requires more than the skill to interact with people in a firm manner.
D. Tact is the only skill that officers use at magnetometer posts.

Answer questions 17 - 18 based on the following "Lost Property Procedure."

Lost Property Procedure

1. Any lost property in the possession of a Police Officer must be delivered by the officer to the "Lost Property Office" in the precinct by the end of the Officer's tour of the day.

2. The Lost Property Officer must inventory the property and safeguard it according to the requirements in the "Property Safeguarding Manual."

3. Property not claimed within 30 days shall be delivered by the Lost Property Officer to the "Central Lost Property Office" at One Police Plaza.

4. If the article is not claimed within one year following the delivery to the "Central Lost Property Office" at One Police Plaza, the article must be sold at auction pursuant to "Lost Property Auction Rules."

5. Funds collected at the auction, net of expenses, must be forwarded by the Central Lost Property Officer to the New York City Finance Administrator.

-----

17. Officer Rolands receives a copy of the above "Lost Property Procedure" the same day in which a pedestrian hands him a diamond ring which he has found on the sidewalk. Officer Rolands used to work in a jewelry store and believes the ring to be costume jewelry. There is one hour remaining before Officer Roland's daily tour ends. Which of the following statements is correct procedure?

A. Officer Rolands should return the ring to the pedestrian and tell him it is costume jewelry.

B. Officer Rolands should take the ring to a jewelry store and have it examined before the end of his tour.

C. Officer Rolands should take the ring to the precinct's "Lost Property Office" before the end of his tour.

D. Officer Rolands should hold on to the ring for at least the following day and have it examined before wasting time delivering it to the "Lost Property Office."

----

18. After the passage of one year from the date property is delivered to the "Central Lost Property Office," the property:

A. must be returned to the precinct Lost Property Office.

B. must be forwarded to the office of the New York City Finance Administrator.

C. must be sold at auction pursuant to "Lost Property Auction Rules, 2014."

D. may be returned to the officer who found the property.

Answer question 19 based on the following "Media Inquiry Procedure."

Media Inquiry Procedure

When a criminal case is pending in the courts, the Police Officer who made the arrest is prohibited from discussing the case with any newspaper, magazine, TV reporters and all other media. Exceptions to this are cases where:

1. a New York court of competent jurisdiction formally orders the Police Officer to discuss one or more particulars of the case.

2. a NYPD authorized Department orders such discussion

3. the Police Officer is subpoenaed to testify by an authorized NYC, NYS, or federal board.

In all cases, media inquiries made to the officer should be referred to HQ Media Services at One Police Plaza.

-----

19. Police Officer Jane Hollis arrests a drug suspect and confiscates two pounds of heroin. The suspect has been indicted and is in jail, waiting for trial. A newspaper reporter, Abigail Briggs, contacts Officer Jane Hollis and asks a quick question, the answer to which might help the reporter to investigate drug trafficking in the city. Officer Jane Hollis should:

A. Answer the question since it is a quick question.

B. Tell the reporter to contact her sergeant.

C. Answer the question only if the reporter is trustworthy.

D. tell the reporter to contact HQ Media Services at One Police Plaza.

Answer question 20 based on the following section of CPL 110.10

CPL 110.10 How to require defendant's appearance for arraignment in a local criminal court

Prior to the commencement of a criminal action, a person may be compelled to appear in a local criminal court for arraignment upon an accusatory instrument to be filed at or before his appearance by:

 (a) an arrest made without a warrant (CPL 140), or

 (b) issuance and service upon him of an appearance ticket (CPL 150).

-----

20. Based on CPL 110.10, which of the following statements is not correct?

A. A person may be compelled to appear in a Local Criminal Court for arraignment upon an accusatory instrument to be filed at or before his appearance by an arrest made without a warrant (CPL 140), or issuance and service upon him of an appearance ticket (CPL 150).

B. A person cannot be compelled to appear in a criminal court prior to the commencement of a criminal action.

C. A person may be compelled to appear in a Local Criminal Court for arraignment upon an accusatory instrument to be filed at or before his appearance by an arrest made without a warrant.

D. A person may be compelled to appear in a Local Criminal Court for arraignment upon an accusatory instrument to be filed at or before his appearance by the issuance and service upon him of an appearance ticket (CPL 150).

Answer questions 21 - 22 on the basis of the following "Building Bomb Search Procedure," received by Police Officer Wells.

Building Bomb Search Procedure

1. Officers will be assigned to search specified areas.
2. If a suspicious object is found:
    a. do not touch the object
    b. keep the area clear of other people
    c. inform security headquarters
3. Be prepared to evacuate all others and yourself.
4. When instructed by security headquarters, evacuate the building according to instructions.
5. Request all persons to take with them all personal belongings when evacuating.

-----

21. Officer Wells is assigned to do a bomb search of the first floor of a three-story paint and household items store. Halfway through his search, he discovers a very suspicious package under a display counter. He listens and hears a distinct ticking sound. There are four other persons on the first floor. Based on the above "Building Bomb Search Procedure," Officer Wells should first:

A. instruct all persons to gather their belongings, as he is about to report the suspicious package and an evacuation may be necessary.
B. issue an evacuation order, as the bomb is ticking and could go off at any second.
C. take the package and put it in an unoccupied section of the store to avoid fatalities.
D. Keep the area clear of other people and inform security headquarters.

----

22. According to the preceding "Building Bomb Search Procedure":

A. When a police officer is instructed by security headquarters to evacuate the building, the officer must request that all persons take with them all personal and <u>business</u> belongings when evacuating.
B. An officer shall never evacuate himself or herself from the building.
C. If a suspicious object is found, the police officer must inform security headquarters.
D. All officers are assigned to search <u>all</u> areas of the building.

----

23. During a city marathon, one of the participants was robbed by a spectator. Four runners stated that they witnessed the robbery. The four runners voluntarily described the suspects with the following statements.

Runner 1: There were two of them, one male and one female, both wearing light jackets. The guy was around 5'10" and the woman was about 5'6". He was muscular, but she looked very slender. Both were wearing blue jeans. His were dark and hers were light. They had on white sneakers and no glasses. He was probably around 190 pounds. She was probably around 125 pounds.

Runner 2: A man and a woman did the robbery. The guy was big and she was the skinny, shorter type. He was about 5'9". I think he had dark hair and she had dirty blonde hair. Both were wearing some type of thin jackets, the windbreaker type, and blue jeans. I would say he was about 170-180 pounds. She was probably around 120-140 pounds. I didn't notice the shoes.

Runner 3: The guy was medium size, like the woman. Both were about 5'6". She had dark hair, not too long, and he had brown or black hair. They were both wearing sneakers, white, I think. They were about the same height, and they were wearing khaki colored pants. I think they were both wearing sweaters.

Runner 4: I didn't get a very good look at them, but one was a guy and one was a woman. They were both under 6 feet, and she was about five inches shorter than him. She was a blonde. I think he had dark brown hair. What I remember most is their thin jackets. I think both jackets had some type of logo on the front chest pocket. He was around 180 and she 140. Both wore jeans.

Trooper Frank Perez is assigned to review the statements of the four witnesses. Based on the preceding information supplied by the four witnesses, Officer Perez should conclude that there is a problem with the description that was provided by witness number:

A. 1   C. 3
B. 2   D. 4

----

24. Officer Parson stops his patrol car at the scene of an auto accident. He sees one car with extensive damage, but no other car that might have been involved in the accident. The driver is on a stretcher and is being attended to by EMS personnel. Four witnesses to the accident inform Officer Parson that the driver of the other vehicle got out of his car for less than a minute and then returned to his car and sped away. The four witnesses all provided a statement to Officer Parson. They described the suspect as follows:

Witness 1: I saw the man. He looked intoxicated. He was slender, around 150 pounds. He had dark hair and was wearing dark pants and black shoes. He was about 5'8".

Witness 2: He was about 6 feet tall and thin, I think. He walked unevenly. He must have weighed no more than 160 pounds. He had dark brown hair and had on black shoes. Like I said, he walked unevenly, like there was something wrong with him.

Witness 3: The man was shaky. He was about 5'7" and skinny. He had dark brown hair and black shoes. He must have weighed about 150 pounds.

Witness 4: The guy was about 5'8" tall. He had light hair and average build. He was probably around 190 pounds. He didn't say anything.

Trooper Frank Perez is assigned to review the statements of the four witnesses. Based on the preceding information supplied by the four witnesses, Officer Perez should conclude that there is a problem with the description that was provided by witness number:

A. 1   C. 3
B. 2   D. 4

Answer Question 25 based on the following table of PL 70.05

PL 70.05 MAXIMUM SENTENCE OF IMPRISONMENT FOR JUVENILE OFFENDER

TYPE OF CONVICTION	MAXIMUM TERM OF IMPRISONMENT
Type "A" felony (murder second degree)	life imprisonment
Type "A" felony (arson first degree or kidnapping first degree)	at least 12, but not more than 15 years
Type "B" felony	10 years
Type "C" felony	7 years
Type "D" felony	4 years

25. According to the preceding table, which of the following choices is a correct maximum term of imprisonment for conviction of the stated offense?

A. Murder in the second degree committed by a Juvenile Offender (maximum 15 years)

B. "C" felony committed by a Juvenile Offender (maximum 10 years)

C. "B" felony committed by a Juvenile Offender (at least 12 nor more than 15 years)

D. "C" felony committed by Juvenile Offender (7 years)

Answer Question 26 based on the following summary of CPL 120.10

CPL 120.10 Warrant of arrest definition, function, form, and content

1. A warrant of arrest is issued by a local criminal court after the filing of an accusatory instrument for the purpose of arraignment. It directs a police officer or designated peace officers to arrest a defendant and bring him to court for arraignment.

2. It is signed by the issuing judge and must state the following:

  (a) name of issuing court,

  (b) date of issuance of the warrant,

  (c) name of offense(s) charged in the accusatory instrument,

  (d) name of defendant to be arrested (or alias or description),

  (e) police or peace officer(s) to whom warrant is addressed,

  (f) direction that officer arrest defendant and bring him to court.

3. A warrant of arrest may be addressed to an individual police officer or classification of officers.

Multiple copies of a warrant may be issued.

-----

26. According to CPL 120.10, which of the following statements is correct?

A. A warrant of arrest must contain the date of the issuance of the warrant.

B. A warrant of arrest must have the signature of the D.A.

C. A warrant of arrest directs that the officer bring the defendant to the local penitentiary.

D. For privacy reasons, a warrant of arrest cannot contain the name of the defendant.

Answer Question 27 based on the following summary of CPL 170.55

CPL 170.55 Adjournment in contemplation of dismissal (ACD)

After arraignment and before entry of plea of guilty or commencement of trial, the court MAY upon motion of the people or defendant, or upon its own motion and consent of both the people and the defendant, order an ACD (ADJOURNMENT IN CONTEMPLATION OF DISMISSAL).

The case is adjourned without a date. People may make an application to restore the case within 6 months. If that occurs, the court may restore it and proceed to trial. If the case is not restored, the accusatory instrument is deemed to have been dismissed in furtherance of justice at the end of the six-month period.

In case of a family offense, the ACD is for 1 year. The people may make an application to restore the case within 1 year.

The court can impose conditions (performance of public service, counseling, etc.) as part of an ACD.

An ACD is NOT a conviction or admission of guilt.

-----

27. According to CPL 170.55, which of the following statements is not correct?

A. An ACD is not an admission of guilt.

B. An ACD in a family offense proceeding is for one year.

C. When an ACD is ordered, the case is adjourned without a date.

D. The people must in all cases consent to the ordering of an ACD by the judge.

Answer questions 28-29 based on the following highlights of "CPL 500.10: Definitions."

CPL 500.10: Definitions

SECURED BAIL BOND is a bond secured by:

1) personal property greater than or equal to the undertaking, or

2) real property at least 2 times the value of the undertaking (assessed value divided by equalization rate, or special assessing unit as defined in article 18 of real property tax law).

PARTIALLY SECURED BAIL BOND is a bond secured by a deposit of money not in excess of 10 per cent of the total amount of the undertaking.

UNSECURED BAIL BOND is a bail bond (other than an insurance company bail bond) that is not secured by any deposit or lien.

-----

28. Which of the following is an example of an unsecured bail bond?

A. a bail bond secured by a deposit of money not in excess of 10 per cent of the total amount of the undertaking

B. a bail bond secured by personal property greater than or equal to undertaking

C. a bail bond (other than an insurance company bail bond) that is not secured by any deposit or lien

D. a bond secured by real property at least 2 times the value of the undertaking

----

29. A bail bond secured by a deposit of money not in excess of 10 per cent of the total amount of the undertaking is a:

A. secured bail bond.

B. unsecured bail bond.

C. questionable secured bail bond.

D. partially secured bail bond.

Answer question 30 based on the following PL 80.05 table.

PL 80.05 FINES FOR MISDEMEANORS AND VIOLATIONS:

Offense	Fine	Alternative Sentence
A misdemeanor	up to $1000.00	Court may sentence the defendant to pay an amount not exceeding double the amount of the defendant's gain.
B misdemeanor	up to $500.00	
Unclassified Misdemeanor	in accordance with law or ordinance that defines the crime	
Violation	up to $250.00	

30. Without regard to defendant's gains, which of the following statements is correct?

A. Fines for violations can only be $25.00 or less.

B. Fines for all misdemeanors must be over $500.

C. Fines for all B misdemeanors must be $500 or more.

D. Fine for an "A" misdemeanor cannot be greater than $1,000.00

Answer question 31 based on the following CPL 30.30 table.

CPL 30.30 Where a defendant has been committed to the custody of the sheriff, he must be released on bail or his own recognizance where the people are not ready for trial within the following days after commencement of defendant's commitment to the custody of the sheriff:

Offense committed	People must be ready for trial within this period (after the commencement of defendant's commitment to the custody of the sheriff)
felony	90 days
misdemeanor with jail term over 3 months	30 days
misdemeanor with jail term up to 3 months	15 days
petty offense	5 days

31. Based on the above table, where the defendant has been committed to the custody of the sheriff and the charge is a petty offense, the people must be ready for trial within _____ days after the commencement of defendant's commitment to the custody of the sheriff.

A. 15 days

B. 5 days

C. 90 days

D. 30 days

Answer questions 32 based on the definitions provided in the following summary of Penal Law Section 10.00.

Penal Law (PL) S 10.00

A **Traffic infraction** is an offense defined as a traffic infraction in section 155 of the Vehicle and Traffic Law.

A **Violation** is an offense (other than a traffic infraction) for which a sentence in excess of 15 days cannot be imposed.

A **Misdemeanor** is an offense (other than a traffic infraction) for which a sentence of more than 15 days and up to and including a year can be imposed.

A **Felony** is an offense for which a sentence of more than 1 year can be imposed.

A **Crime** means a misdemeanor or a felony.

Physical injury means impairment of physical condition or substantial pain.

Serious physical injury means physical injury which creates a substantial risk of death, or which causes death or serious and protracted disfigurement, protracted impairment of health or protracted loss or impairment of the function of any bodily organ.

Deadly physical force means physical force which under the circumstances used is readily capable of causing death or other serious physical injury.

Deadly weapon means any loaded weapon from which a shot, readily capable of producing death or other serious physical injury, may be discharged, or any of the following: switchblade knife, gravity knife, pilum ballistic knife, metal knuckle knife, dagger, billy, blackjack, plastic knuckles, metal knuckles.

Dangerous instrument means any instrument, including a vehicle, which is readily capable of causing death or other serious physical injury.

-----

32. Based on the definitions in the above summary of Penal Law 10.00, which of the following statements is correct?

A. A sentence of 13 months may be imposed for a misdemeanor.

B. Traffic infractions are defined in the Penal Law.

C. A sentence of 360 days may be imposed for a misdemeanor.

D. Deadly weapons and dangerous instruments have the same definition.

Answer questions 33 - 34 based on the following extracts of CPL 500.10.

CPL 500.10 Definitions

1. PRINCIPAL is a defendant in a criminal action, or person adjudged to be a material witness.

2. RELEASE ON OWN RECOGNIZANCE means to allow a principal to be at liberty during pendency of an action.

3. TO FIX BAIL means a court designating a sum of money, the posting of which allows the principal to be at liberty during the pendency of the criminal action.

4. COMMIT TO THE CUSTODY OF THE SHERIFF occurs when a court orders a principal confined and in the custody of the sheriff during the pendency of the criminal action.

5. SECURING ORDER is a court order which:

     1) commits a principal to custody of the sheriff, or

     2) fixes bail, or

     3) releases the principal on his own recognizance.

-----

33. Which of the following statements is correct?

A. A person can be committed to the custody of the sheriff only if he is a defendant in a criminal action.

B. If a defendant posts bail, he cannot be released.

C. A "principal" can only be a defendant in an action.

D. If a person is released on his own recognizance, he can remain at liberty during the pendency of the criminal action.

----

34. According to the definitions in CPL 500.10, which of the following statements is correct?

A. A principal means only a defendant in a criminal action.

B. A securing order cannot order the release of the principal on his own recognizance.

C. A judge cannot designate a sum of money when posting bail.

D. A securing order can order the release of the principal in his own recognizance.

----

35. Four witnesses to a hit and run accident tell Police Officer Tumi that they memorized the license plate number of the car that sped away from the accident. Which of the following is the most likely to be correct?

A. 8237AFN   C. 8537AFN

B. 8587AFN   D. 8531AFN

Answer question 36 based on the following table.

Summonses and Desk Appearance Tickets Issued by Police Officer Wooster

Week	Dates	Parking Summonses	Moving Summonses	Desk Appearance Tickets
1	Sept 1 – 7	14	15	3
2	Sept 8 -14	11	3	6
3	Sept 15 -21	16	10	1
4	Sept 22 – 28	9	12	5
5	Sept 29 – Oct 5	18	11	7

36. Police Officer Wooster is adding up the total number of summonses and Desk Appearance Tickets issued by her during the above five-week period. Which of the following four formulas should she use to arrive at the correct number of summonses that she issued?

A. 18+11+7

B. 3+6+1+5+7

C. 14+11+16+9+18+15+3+10+12+11+3+6+1+5+7

D. 1(14+11+16+9+18) + 2(15+3+10+12+11) + 3(3+6+1+5+7)

----

37. Police Officer Hanson is assigned to patrol an area which includes four public parks. During the prior four weeks, crime statistics show that four muggings were reported at the Jackson Park, all between the hours of 10:00 a.m. and 4:00 p.m. At the Washington Park six purse snatchings were reported. At the Bellmore Park eight strollers were stolen. At the Green Valley Park four bicycles were stolen. The muggings all occurred between 9:30 a.m. and 4:30 p.m. The purse snatchings occurred between 9:30 a.m. and 10:30 a.m. The strollers were stolen in the afternoon and before 3:00 p.m.

Officer Hanson works the 9:00 a.m. to 5:00 p.m. tour. On Monday, his sergeant instructs him to pay careful attention to stroller robberies. To try to reduce the number of stroller robberies, Office Hanson should patrol:

A. Washington Park

B. Green Valley Park

C. Bellmore Park

D. Green Valley Park and Washington Park

38. On Tuesday Officer Hanson works the 9:00 a.m. to 5:00 p.m. tour. His sergeant tells him that six bicycles have been stolen at the same park where four bicycles were stolen during the prior four weeks. To try to reduce the number of bicycles being stolen, Officer Hanson should patrol:

A. Washington Park

C. Bellmore Park

B. Green Valley Park

D. Columbus Park

----

39. While you are on patrol, a female, about 50 years old, reports that she had left her pet dog in her unlocked car, with the window open, and gone into a pet store to purchase dog food, only to discover when she came out of the store that her car had been stolen. You question four witnesses who give you four statements. Which of the following four statements is most likely to be incorrect?

A. The person who drove the car away was a male, white, about 30 years old and about six feet tall. He was wearing black sneakers, grey sweat pants, and a backpack. He drove the car for one block and then made a right turn.

B. The person drove away was a male, white, about six feet tall. He was wearing black sneakers, blue dungarees, a blue yellow T-shirt, and a dark brown backpack. He drove north for one block and then made a left turn.

C. The person who robbed the car was a male, white, about six feet tall. He was wearing black sneakers, blue dungarees, a T-shirt, and a dark brown backpack. He drove away and then made a left.

D. The car robber was a male, white. I'm not sure how tall he was. He was wearing black sneakers, blue dungarees, a yellow T-shirt, and a dark brown backpack. I didn't notice which direction he went.

----

40. Four witnesses to a hit and run accident tell Police Officer Tumi that they memorized the license plate of the car that sped away from the accident. Which of the following is the most like to be correct?

A. 4237AKL

C. 4537AKL

B. 4587AKL

D. 4531SAKL

Answer questions 41-42 based on the following "Building Smoking Procedure."

Building Smoking Procedure

1. Smoking in a NYS government building is not permitted, except in designated areas.
2. A member of the public who is found to be smoking in an area where smoking is not permitted must be asked by the NYS Trooper to extinguish what he is smoking.
3. If the person refuses to do so, the officer shall remove the person from the facility, and if the person resists, the Officer may charge the person with the appropriate violation of law.
4. A NYS employee found to be smoking in an area where smoking is not permitted must be asked by the Officer to extinguish what he is smoking, and if the employee refuses, the Correction Officer must file an unusual incident report which will subject the employee to disciplinary charges.

-----

41. NYS Trooper Ben Donaldson sees a person smoking in a hallway of a NYS government building. He informs the person that smoking is not permitted. The person tells Officer Donaldson that he disagrees, and that he is a NYS employee and therefore is allowed to smoke in the building. Based on the above "Building Smoking Procedure", which of the following is a correct action for Trooper Donaldson to take?

A. He files an unusual incident report because he has found a member of the public smoking in a NYS government building.

B. Because the person smoking is a NYS employee, he charges the person with the appropriate violation of NYS law.

C. Trooper Donaldson does nothing because he knows that in reality, smoking is permitted in fifty per cent of NYS government buildings.

D. He files an unusual incident report because the person is a NYS employee who is smoking in an area where smoking is not permitted and is resisting a lawful order to stop smoking.

----

42. NYS Trooper Karen Lam sees a member of the public smoking in a NYS government building. Which of the following is the next correct action for Officer Lam to take?

A. Immediately arrest the person for violating the law.

B. Remove the person from the facility, as smoking is not permitted in NYS government buildings.

C. File an unusual incident report.

D. Inform the person that smoking is not permitted in NYS government buildings.

Question 43

The following are 5 sentences (in random order) relating to Staffing of Magnetometers posts.

1. Finally, the officer must be in possession of the biohazard gear issued to each officer by the NYS Trooper Academy.

2. The MP-P2017 certificate must have been signed by the HNY Officer who administered the training and must be embossed with the NYS seal (NYS-S2017).

3. Troopers assigned to magnetometer posts must have completed the required training.

4. In addition to the MP-P2017 certificate with the NYS seal, a 5626GHT waiver, signed by the officer, must be on file.

5. First, each officer must produce the certificate of successful completion of Training (MP-P2017).

43. Choose the best logical order of sentences from the following four choices:

A. 3 - 5 - 2 - 1 - 4   **C. 3 - 5 - 2 - 4 - 1**

B. 2 - 5 - 3 - 4 - 1   D. A. 5 - 3 - 2 - 4 - 1

Questions 44 - 45

Procedure for a Cell Search

1. After learning which cell you are to search, collect the necessary materials to do the search (flashlight, mirror, protective gloves, etc.)
2. Instruct the offender to come out of the cell and perform a pat on the offender before having another NYS Trooper escort him to the day room, where he is to wait until the search of the cell is completed.
3. Search the cell. Be careful of dangerous sharp objects or other hazards. Look over, under and behind everything.
4. If you find any contraband, place it in one area of the cell and continue the search until completed.
5. After you have completed the search of the cell, fill-out a "Cell Contraband Form 100-2017" and prepare all other forms, including "Disciplinary Recommendation Form 3-G).
6. Check-in all confiscated property to the Detained Suspect Property Room.

-----

44. Trooper Melkowitz is assigned to do a search of a cell occupied by a suspect. Based on the above, which of the following statements is the first step that Trooper Melkowitz should carry out?

A. Pat-down the inmate before he goes out of his cell.

B. Look for contraband and immediately remove it from the cell.

C. Complete Contraband Form 100-2071.

D. Instruct the offender to come out of the cell.

----

45. During his search, Trooper Melkowitz discovers a bayonet inside the mattress of the suspect. According to the "Procedure for a Cell Search," what is the action first action that Trooper Melkowitz should take?
A. Immediately question the suspect regarding the bayonet.

B. Ask the suspects in the adjacent cells if they know anything about the bayonet.

C. Immediately report the bayonet to his sergeant so that he may take appropriate action.

D. Place the bayonet in one area of the cell and continue the search of the cell.

Questions 46-48

Security Classification of Inmates

The following are rules to be followed to classify for security purposes each inmate upon temporary incarceration at a NYS Trooper facility:
1. A misdemeanor offender admitted to this facility shall be assigned a security code Level A.
2. A felony offender sentenced to more than 12 months and less than 37 months shall be assigned a security code level of Level B.
3. A felony offender sentenced to more than 36 months and up to and including 360 months shall be assigned a security code of Level C.

4. A felon offender sentenced to more than 360 months and up to and including life in prison shall be assigned a security code of Level D.

Use the following situation and the above rules to answer Questions 46-48:
A NYS Trooper is assigned to review for correctness the security codes of the prisoners in Unit 7H (a Unit that is equipped to handle security Level C inmates). As a result of his review, he finds out the following about the assigned security codes of the following inmates in Unit 7H.
- James Sumpter, a newly processed felony offender, is serving a sentence of 262 months.
- Victor Arbor, a newly processed felony offender, is serving a sentence of 4 years.
- Charles Youngs, a newly processed felony offender, is serving a sentence of 30 years and 2 months.
- David Peterson, a newly processed felony offender, is serving a sentence of 3 years and 5 months.

----

46. Based on the above, which of the following statements is true?

A. All the inmates are in their correct security code Level C unit (Unit 7H)

B. Victor Arbor and Charles Youngs are the only two inmates that are in their correct security code Level C Unit.

C. None of the inmates are in their correct security code Level C Unit.

D. Charles Youngs is not in his correct security code Level C Unit.

----

47. Which of the above four inmates is serving the least sentence?

A. James Sumpter   C. Charles Youngs

B. Victor Arbor   D. David Peterson

----

48. A felon offender sentenced to 35 years shall be assigned security code level "C."
A. True in all cases.
B. False.
C. True, only if the felony offender is over the age of 21.
D. True, if the felony offender is male.
A felon offender sentenced to more than 360 months (30 years) and up to and including life in prison shall be assigned a security code of Level D.

END OF PRACTICE TEST QUESTIONS

----

11. PRACTICE TEST ANSWERS

1. What is the time of the accident?
A. 9:50 p.m.   **C. 9:45 p.m.**
B. 10:15 p.m.   D. before 9:30 a.m.
(The passage states, "…at 9:45 p.m. they witnessed a minor traffic accident….")

2. How many persons were injured as a result of the traffic accident?
A. 1   C. 2
B. 0   D. none of the above
(The passage states, "…the two drivers, and two passengers (one in each vehicle) did not sustain any personal injuries….")

3. Which car sustained extensive damage to the driver's side front door?
A.   NY plate #607PHB, black 2012 Ford Edge
B.   NY plate #4357ZN, black 2012 Ford Edge
C.   NY plate #4357ZN, blue 2011 Ford Escape
D.   NY plate #607PHB, blue 2011 Ford Escape
(The passage states, "…vehicle driven by a male named Mark Levington, had extensive damage to the driver's door…Mr. Levington's auto was a blue 2011 Ford Escape, NY license plate 607PHB.")

4. Which of the following statements is not correct?
A. The auto driven by Felix Upton, age 46, was a black 2012 Ford Edge.
B. The vehicle Accident Report number was 4839274732.
(The correct Accident Report number is 48392747332.)
C. Mark Levington, age 52, resides at 2686 Manor Street, Brooklyn, N.Y.
D. Mr. Upton's N.Y. driver's license identification number is D274 43 662.

5. Which of the following is correct?
A. The person residing at 1942 West 58th Street, New York, N.Y. has a N.Y. driver's license identification number D274 43 66**5** with an expiration date of December 31, 2016.
(WRONG. The correct driver's license identification number D274 43 66**2**.)
B. Mark Levington, age **25**, resides at 2686 Manor Street, Brooklyn, N.Y.
(WRONG. "The driver of the other auto was Mark Levington, age 52….)
C. The auto driven by Felix Upton, is a black 2012 Ford Edge, N.Y. license plate 4357ZB.
(CORRECT. "The auto driven by Felix Upton, age 46, was a black 2012 Ford Edge, N.Y. license plate 4357ZB.)
D. The accident occurred at East 16th Street and Kings Highway in the Bronx.
(WRONG. "…they witnessed a minor traffic accident at East 16th Street and Kings Highway in Brooklyn.)

6. Police Officer Marino, a NYPD Officer assigned to a precinct in Queens County, has in his possession a warrant of arrest issued by a district court for a person named Jack Wringer. Which of the following choices is correct?

A. Police Officer Marino cannot execute the warrant of arrest because it was issued by a district court and not a New York City court.

(WRONG. A warrant of arrest issued by a <u>district court</u> can be executed <u>anywhere in the state</u>.)

B. Jack Wringer cannot be arrested on that warrant if he is outside the county served by the district court.

(WRONG. A warrant of arrest issued by a <u>district court</u> can be executed <u>anywhere in the state</u>.)

C. Police Officer Marino may execute the warrant outside the state of New York.

(WRONG. A warrant of arrest issued by a <u>district court</u>, NYC criminal court or a superior court judge sitting as a local criminal court can be executed <u>anywhere in the state</u>.)

D. Police Officer Marino may execute the warrant because it was issued by a district court.

(CORRECT. A warrant of arrest issued by <u>a district court</u>, NYC criminal court or a superior court judge sitting as a local criminal court can be executed <u>anywhere in the state</u>.)

7. Police Officer Jane Goodwin, a NYPD Officer assigned to a precinct in Brooklyn, has in her possession a warrant of arrest issued by a town court in Nassau County. Which of the following statements is correct?

A. Officer Goodwin can execute the warrant in Brooklyn.

B. Officer Goodwin can execute the warrant only on weekdays in Brooklyn.

C. Officer Goodwin can execute the warrant in Brooklyn only if it has the written endorsement of a local criminal court of the county in which the arrest is to be made, in this case, Kings County (Brooklyn).

(CORRECT. A warrant of arrest issued by a city, town, or village court can be executed in the county of issuance or adjoining county, <u>or anywhere in NYS upon the written endorsement of a local criminal court of the county in which arrest is to be made</u>).

D. Officer Goodwin can execute the warrant in New Jersey.

8. According to CPL 120.70, which of the following is not correct?

A. A warrant of arrest issued by a superior court judge sitting as a local criminal court can be executed anywhere in the state.

B. A warrant of arrest issued by the NYC criminal court can be executed anywhere in the state.

C. A warrant of arrest issued by the board of a school district can be executed anywhere in the state.

(CPL 120.70 does not address warrants of arrest issued by the board of a <u>school</u> district. Therefore, this statement is not correct.)

D. Some warrants of arrest may be executed anywhere in the state.

9. A. Send backup to the corner of Jefferson and 66th Street. Received a report that there are two bombers with backpacks in the vicinity. One has a black backpack and the other has a grey backpack with logos on them. Suggest you stop anyone with a backpack.

(This is not the best choice. It leaves out important ID details, such as the approximate ages of the two men, the type of logos on the backpacks, the fact that they were overheard discussing detonating bombs, and the approximate time that the witness overheard the bombers.)

B. "Possible bomber situation. Several minutes ago, two men in their 20's were overheard planning to detonate bombs during the parade. Suspect number one has black hair and is shouldering a black backpack with a united states flag logo. Suspect number two has blonde hair and a grey backpack with a peace symbol logo. Last seen several minutes ago, walking on Jefferson toward 66."
(**This is the best choice.** It includes all the vital information that should be transmitted to control.)
C. Bomber situation. Two men were overheard planning to detonate bombs during the parade. Suspect number one has black hair and is shouldering a black backpack with a united states flag logo. Suspect number two has black hair and a grey backpack with a peace symbol logo. Last seen walking on Jefferson toward 66."
(**This is not the best choice.** It leaves out even more detail than choice "A.")
D. "Bomb alert. Two men wearing backpacks who were talking about exploding them. They are heading toward 66th Street. Suggest you stop and frisk them. The report is from a young woman."
(**This is not the best choice.** Like choices "A" and "C" it is almost devoid of the important facts.)

Answer 10. (D) 5-4-3-2-1
5. The manner and length of time that one practices answering questions can greatly affect the mark that one receives on an exam.
4. Short study sessions over a long period of time are very helpful.
3. Short sessions help the brain retain more, while studying over a period of time help to reinforce the neural connections in the brain.
2. This does not mean, however, that all neural connections and all brains work alike.
1. Everyone is different, and there may be as many ways to study as there are people.

Answer 11: (B) 5-4-1-3-2
(5) Some open competitive civil service exams for positions in the court system do not include legal definitions.
(4) They are designed to test general knowledge and aptitude only.
(1) They are restricted to these two outward aims because to test legal expertise would be unfair to the general public.
(3) A third, invisible aim, therefore, is fairness.
(2) This aim is probably the most important and merit worthy aspect of civil service exams.

12. Officer Nordstrum is preparing a report of the accident and has four drafts of the report. He wishes to use the draft that expresses the information most clearly, accurately and completely. Which draft should he choose?

A. At 4:15 p.m., on September 9, 2016, at the intersection of Lavin Avenue and Reiker Avenue, Bronx, a vehicle driven by Barry Jones struck a commercial metal garbage container protruding into the street.
(**WRONG.** Type of vehicle, <u>a 2008 Toyota Sienna</u>, is not stated.)

B. On September 9, 2016, at 4:15 p.m., at the intersection of Lavin Avenue and Reiker Avenue, Bronx, a 2008 Toyota Sienna driven by Barry <u>Lones</u> struck a commercial metal garbage container protruding into the street.
(**WRONG.** Jones is misspelled <u>Lones</u>.)

C. On September 9, 2016, at <u>4:25 p.m.</u>, at the intersection of Lavin Avenue and Reiker Avenue, Bronx, a 2008 Toyota Sienna driven by Barry Jones struck a commercial metal garbage container protruding into the street.
(**WRONG.** Time is not correct. Time should be <u>4:15 p.m.</u>)

D. On September 9, 2016, at 4:15 p.m., at the intersection of Lavin Avenue and Reiker Avenue, Bronx, a 2008 Toyota Sienna driven by Barry Jones struck a commercial metal garbage container protruding into the street.
(**BEST DRAFT.** All the information is stated and is accurate.)

13. Officer Nordstrum is comparing the information he recorded in his memo pad (at the scene of the accident) to the information in his report. Which of the above choices (A, B, C, or D) has a detail that does not agree with the information in the officer's memo pad?
A. Date of Accident: September 9, 2016; Time of accident: 4:15 p.m.
B. Place of accident: Intersection of Lavin Avenue and Reiker Avenue, Bronx
C. Driver: Barry Jones: Vehicle: 2008 Toyota Sienna
D. Damage: Vehicle struck a commercial plastic garbage container protruding into the street
(**ONE DETAIL IS WRONG.** The garbage container is <u>metal</u> and not <u>plastic</u>.)

14. Your partner is driving south in your squad patrol car and the squad car is at the intersection of Lincoln St. and Franklin Avenue. You are informed that an auto accident has just occurred at the intersection of Waring Street and Ingersoll Avenue. Assuming you must obey all traffic signs, which one of the following four choices describes the best statement you can give your partner as to the most direct route?
A. Drive south on Franklin Avenue to Fairfield St, then drive east on Fairfield St. to Ingersoll Avenue, then south to the intersection of Dorance Street and Ingersoll Avenue.
B. Drive south on Franklin Avenue to Fairfield St, then drive west on Fairfield St. to Ingersoll Avenue, then north to the intersection of Dorance Street and Ingersoll Avenue.
C. Drive north on Franklin Avenue to Fairfield St, then drive east on Fairfield St. to Ingersoll Avenue, then north to the intersection of Dorance Street and Ingersoll Avenue.
D. Drive south on Franklin Avenue to Fairfield St, then drive west on Fairfield St. to Ingersoll Avenue, then south to the intersection of Waring Street and Ingersoll Avenue.

15. Which of the following statements best reflects the wishes of the sergeant?

A. Please remember that an "Aided" incident report is used to document bomb threats.

B. Keep in mind that "Aided" and "Unusual Occurrence" reports prevent law suits against Court Officers.

C. Please remember that an "Aided" report is filled out if an officer calls for an ambulance for an injured person. An Unusual Incident Report is filled out for non-medical incidents.

(**This is the best choice** because it emphasizes the difference between aided and unusual incident reports, which must be kept in mind to properly select the appropriate report to submit.)

D. Please keep in mind that an "Aided" report, and not an unusual incident report, must be filled out if a person with disabilities is a party in an active case.

16. According to the preceding passage, which of the following possible statements by Officer Holmes best summarizes what Officer Holmes is trying to convey?

A. You are here because all officers should be trained in magnetometer operation.

B. Officers should get at least 8 hours of sleep each night.

C. Staffing a magnetometer post requires more than the skill to interact with people in a firm manner.

D. Tact is the only skill that officers use at magnetometer posts.

17. Which of the following statements is correct procedure?

A. Officer Rolands should return the ring to the pedestrian and tell him it is costume jewelry. (**NOT CORRECT.** This is contrary to the Lost Property Procedure.)

B. Officer Rolands should take the ring to a jewelry store and have it examined before the end of his tour.

(**NOT CORRECT.** This is not one of the stated procedures.)

C. Officer Rolands should take the ring to the precinct's "Lost Property Office" before the end of his tour.

(**CORRECT.** Any lost property in the possession of a Police Officer must be delivered by the Officer to the "Lost Property Office" in the precinct by the end of the Officer's tour of the day.)

D. Officer Rolands should hold on to the ring for at least the following day and have it examined before wasting time delivering it to the "Lost Property Office."

(**NOT CORRECT.** The ring must be delivered to the Lost Property Office before the end of the tour.)

18. After the passage of one year from the date property is delivered to the "Central Lost Property Office," the property:

A. must be returned to the precinct Lost Property Office.

B. must be forwarded to the office of the New York City Finance Administrator.

C. must be sold at auction pursuant to "Lost Property Auction Rules, 2014."

("C" is CORRECT. "4. If the article is not claimed within one year following the delivery to the "Central Lost Property Office" at One Police Plaza, the article must be sold at auction pursuant to "Lost Property Auction Rules, 2014." Choices A, B, and D are contrary to the procedure.)

D. may be returned to the officer who found the property.

19. Officer Jane Hollis should:

A. Answer the question since it is a quick question.

B. Tell the reporter to contact her sergeant.

C. Answer the question only if the reporter is trustworthy.

D. tell the reporter to contact HQ Media Services at One Police Plaza.

(CORRECT. Choices A, B, and C are contrary to the Media Inquiry Procedure.)

20. Based on CPL 110.10, which of the following statements is not correct?

A. A person may be compelled to appear in a Local Criminal Court for arraignment upon an accusatory instrument to be filed at or before his appearance by an arrest made without a warrant (CPL 140), or issuance and service upon him of an appearance ticket (CPL 150).

B. A person cannot be compelled to appear in a criminal court prior to the commencement of a criminal action.

("Prior to the commencement of a criminal action, a person <u>may</u> be compelled to appear....")

C. A person may be compelled to appear in a Local Criminal Court for arraignment upon an accusatory instrument to be filed at or before his appearance by an arrest made without a warrant.

D. A person may be compelled to appear in a Local Criminal Court for arraignment upon an accusatory instrument to be filed at or before his appearance by the issuance and service upon him of an appearance ticket (CPL 150).

21. Based on the above "Building Bomb Search Procedure," Officer Wells should first:

A. instruct all persons to gather their belongings, as he is about to report the suspicious package and an evacuation may be necessary.

B. issue an evacuation order, as the bomb is ticking and could go off at any second.

C. take the package and put it in an unoccupied section of the store to avoid fatalities.

D. keep the area clear of other people and inform security headquarters.

(Steps 2 and 3 state:

"2. If a suspicious object is found:

      a. do not touch the object

      b. keep the area clear of other people

      c. inform security headquarters....")

22. According to the preceding "Building Bomb Search Procedure":

A. When a police officer is instructed by security headquarters to evacuate the building, the officer must request that all persons take with them all personal and <u>business</u> belongings when evacuating.

(WRONG. The procedure refers to <u>personal</u> belongings.)

B. An officer shall never evacuate himself or herself from the building.

(WRONG. An officer must do so when instructed.)

C. If a suspicious object is found, the police officer must inform security headquarters.

(CORRECT. Steps 2 states:

"2. If a suspicious object is found:

     a. do not touch the object

     b. keep the area clear of other people

     <u>c. inform security headquarters</u>....")

D. All officers are assigned to search <u>all</u> areas of the building.

(WRONG. Officers are assigned to search <u>specified</u> areas.)

23. Based on the preceding information supplied by the four witnesses, Officer Perez should conclude that there is a problem with the description that was provided by witness number:

A. 1   **C. 3**

B. 2   D. 4

The answer is C. 3 (witness number 3). (Two other witnesses described the man as "muscular" and the woman as being "slender" or "skinny." Witness three described both as having a "medium build." Also, witness number three described the woman's hair as "dark," whereas the other three witnesses described the hair as "light", "dirty blonde," or just "blond." Finally, all the other witnesses described the pants of both suspects as "jeans," or "blue jeans," whereas witness number three described them as "khaki pants."

24. Based on the preceding information supplied by the four witnesses, Officer Perez should conclude that there is a problem with the description that was provided by witness number:

A. 1   C. 3

B. 2   **D. 4**

The answer for question number 7 is D. 4 (witness number 4). (The three other witnesses described both the man as "slender" or "skinny." Witness 4 described him as being of "average build." Also, witness 4 described the man's hair as "light," whereas the other three described the hair as "dark" or "dark brown." Finally, witness 4 estimated the weights of the man as 190 pounds, which is about 30-40 pounds more than the weights estimated by the other three witnesses.

25. According to the preceding table, which of the following choices is a correct maximum term of imprisonment for conviction of the stated offense?

A. Murder in the second degree committed by a Juvenile Offender (maximum 15 years)

(WRONG. Maximum is <u>life imprisonment</u>.)

B. "C" felony committed by a Juvenile Offender (maximum 10 years)

(WRONG. Maximum is <u>7 years</u>.)

C. "B" felony committed by a Juvenile Offender (at least 12 nor more than 15 years)

(**WRONG.** Maximum is <u>10 years</u>.)

D. "C" felony committed by Juvenile Offender (7 years)

(**CORRECT.** A "C" felony maximum term is <u>7 years</u>.)

26. According to CPL 120.10, which of the following statements is correct?

A. A warrant of arrest must contain the date of the issuance of the warrant.

(**CORRECT.** "A warrant of arrest: 2. It is signed by the issuing judge and must state the following:
  (a) name of issuing court,
  (b) <u>date of issuance of the warrant</u>....)"

B. A warrant of arrest must have the signature of the D.A.

(**WRONG.** "It is signed by the <u>issuing judge</u>.")

C. A warrant of arrest directs that the officer bring the defendant to the local penitentiary.

(**WRONG.** A warrant of arrest directs the officer to bring the defendant to <u>court</u>.)

D. For privacy reasons, a warrant of arrest cannot contain the name of the defendant.

(**WRONG.** A warrant of arrest <u>can</u> contain the name of the defendant, or alias or description.)

27. According to CPL 170.55, which of the following statements is not correct?

A. An ACD is not an admission of guilt.

B. An ACD in a family offense proceeding is for one year.

C. When an ACD is ordered, the case is adjourned without a date.

D. The people must in all cases consent to the ordering of an ACD by the judge.

(**This statement is <u>not</u> correct** because "After arraignment and before entry of plea of guilty or commencement of trial, court <u>may</u> upon motion of people or defendant, or upon its own motion <u>and consent of both the people and the defendant</u>, order an ACD.)

28. Which of the following is an example of an unsecured bail bond?

A. a bail bond secured by a deposit of money not in excess of 10 per cent of the total amount of the undertaking

(**WRONG.** This is the definition of a <u>partially</u> secured bail bond.)

B. a bail bond secured by personal property greater than or equal to undertaking

(**WRONG.** This is the definition of a <u>secured</u> bail bond.)

C. a bail bond (other than an insurance company bail bond) that is not secured by any deposit or lien

(**CORRECT.** This is the definition of an "<u>Unsecured bail bond</u>.")

D. a bond secured by real property at least 2 times the value of the undertaking

(**WRONG.** This is the definition of a <u>secured</u> bail bond.)

29. A bail bond secured by a deposit of money not in excess of 10 per cent of the total amount of the undertaking is a:

A. secured bail bond.

C. questionable secured bail bond.

B. unsecured bail bond.

D. partially secured bail bond.

"PARTIALLY SECURED BAIL BOND is a bond secured by a deposit of money not in excess of 10 per cent of the total amount of the undertaking."

----

30. Without regards to defendant's gain, which of the following statements is correct?

A. Fines for violations can only be $25.00 or less.

(WRONG. Fine can be up to $250.00)

B. Fines for all misdemeanors must be over $500.

(WRONG. Fine for B misdemeanor is up to $500.00)

C. Fines for all B misdemeanors must be $500 or more.

(WRONG. Fine for B misdemeanor is up to $500.00)

D. Fine for an "A" misdemeanor cannot be greater than $1,000.00 (CORRECT)

31. Based on the above table, where the defendant has been committed to the custody of the sheriff and the charge is a petty offense, the people must be ready for trial within _____ days after the commencement of defendant's commitment to the custody of the sheriff.

A. 15 days

C. 90 days

B. 5 days

D. 30 days

32. A. A sentence of 13 months may be imposed for a misdemeanor.

(WRONG. Maximum sentence for a misdemeanor is up to a year.)

B. Traffic infractions are defined in the Penal Law.

(WRONG. Traffic Infractions are defined in the Vehicle and Traffic Law.)

C. A sentence of 360 days may be imposed for a misdemeanor.

(CORRECT. A misdemeanor is an offense (other than a traffic infraction) for which a sentence of more than 15 days and up to and including a year can be imposed. A year is 365 days.)

D. Deadly weapons and dangerous instruments have the same definition.

(WRONG. They have two different definitions.)

33. Which of the following statements is correct?

A. A person can be committed to the custody of the sheriff only if he is a defendant in a criminal action.

(WRONG. A person can also be committed to the custody of the sheriff if he is adjudged to be a <u>material witness</u>.)

B. If a defendant posts bail, he cannot be released.

(WRONG. If a defendant posts bail, he <u>must</u> be released.)

C. A "principal" can only be a defendant in an action.

(WRONG. A "principal" can be a <u>material witness.</u>)

D. If a person is released on his own recognizance, he can remain at liberty during the pendency of the criminal action.

(CORRECT. "2. RELEASE ON OWN RECOGNIZANCE means to allow a principal to be at liberty during the pendency of an action.")

34. According to the definitions in CPL 500.10, which of the following statements is correct?

A. A principal means only a defendant in a criminal action.

(WRONG. A principal can also be a person who is a <u>material witness</u>.)

B. A securing order cannot order the release of the principal on his own recognizance.

(WRONG. A securing order <u>can</u> order the release of the principal on his own recognizance.)

C. A judge cannot designate a sum of money when posting bail.

(WRONG. The <u>judge designates the sum of money</u> to be posted as bail.)

D. A securing order can order the release of the principal in his own recognizance.

(CORRECT. "5. SECURING ORDER is a court order which:

    1) commits a principal to custody of the sheriff, or

    2) fixes bail, or

    3) <u>releases the principal on his own recognizance.</u>")

35. Four witnesses to a hit and run accident tell Police Officer Tumi that they memorized the license plate number of the car that sped away from the accident. Which of the following is the most likely to be correct?

A. 8237AFN   **C. 8537AFN**

B. 8587AFN   D. 8531AFN

Explanation:

The first digit "8" is the same in all choices.

Choice "A" differs from all others in that the second digit is "2" instead of "5." We can eliminate "A".

Choice "B" differs from the remaining by having an "8" as the third digit instead of "3." This leaves choices "C" and" D."

Choice "D" differs from the other choices in that the fourth digit is "1" instead of "7."
The best choice is therefore **"C. 8537AFN"**

36. Police Officer Wooster is adding up the total number of summonses and Desk Appearance Tickets issued by her during the above five-week period. Which of the following four formulas should she use to arrive at the correct number of summonses that she issued?

A. 18+11+7
(**WRONG because this totals only the summonses issued Sept 29 – Oct 5.**)
B. 3+6+1+5+7
(**WRONG because this only totals the Desk Appearance Tickets issued.**)
C. 14+11+16+9+18+15+3+10+12+11+3+6+1+5+7
(**CORRECT.** This correctly includes all the summonses and Desk Appearance Tickets, a total of 141.)
D. 1(14+11+16+9+18) + 2(15+3+10+12+11) + 3(3+6+1+5+7)
(**WRONG** because this is a mathematical formula which multiplies each parenthetical group of summonses and Desk Appearance Tickets issued by the number preceding the parenthesis. The total would be 236.)

37. To try to reduce the number of stroller robberies, Office Hanson should patrol:

A. Washington Park
B. Green Valley Park
C. Bellmore Park
("At the Bellmore Park eight <u>strollers</u> were stolen" during the prior four weeks.)
D. Green Valley Park and Washington Park

38. To try to reduce the number of bicycles being stolen, Officer Hanson should patrol:

A. Washington Park
B. Green Valley Park
("At the Green Valley Park four <u>bicycles</u> were stolen" during the prior four weeks.)
C. Bellmore Park
D. Columbus Park

----

39. Which of the following four statements is most likely to be incorrect?

A. The person who drove the car away was a male, white, about 30 years old and about six feet tall. He was wearing black sneakers, **grey sweat pants,** and a backpack. He drove the car for one block and then made a **right turn.**

(**Most likely to be incorrect. This is the only witness who described the pants as "grey sweat pants" instead of blue dungarees. Also, he said the robber turned right instead of left.**

B. The person drove away was a male, white, about six feet tall. He was wearing black sneakers, **blue dungarees**, a blue yellow T-shirt, and a dark brown backpack. He drove north for one block and then made **a left turn.**

C. The person who robbed the car was a male, white, about six feet tall. He was wearing black sneakers, **blue dungarees**, a T-shirt, and a dark brown backpack. He drove away and then made a left.

D. The car robber was a male, white. I'm not sure how tall he was. He was wearing black sneakers, **blue dungarees**, a yellow T-shirt, and a dark brown backpack. I didn't notice which direction he went.

40. Four witnesses to a hit and run accident tell Police Officer Tumi that they memorized the license plate of the car that sped away from the accident. Which of the following is the most likely to be correct?

A. 4237AKL

Choice "A" is <u>not</u> the most likely to be correct because the second numeral "2" differs from the "5" of the other three choices.

B. 4587AKL

Choice "B" is also <u>not</u> the most likely to be correct because the third numeral "8" differs from the "3" of the other three choices.

C. 4537AKL

(Choice "C" is the most likely to be correct. This is the plate number whose numerals agree with most other plate numbers.)

D. 4531AKL

Choice "D" is also <u>not</u> the most likely to be correct because the fourth numeral "1" differs from the "7" of the other three choices.**)**

41. Based on the above "Building Smoking Procedure", which of the following is a correct action for Trooper Donaldson to take?

A. He files an unusual incident report because he has found a member of the public smoking in a NYS government building.

B. Because the person smoking is a NYS employee, he charges the person with the appropriate violation of NYS law.

C. Trooper Donaldson does nothing because he knows that in reality, smoking is permitted in fifty per cent of NYS government buildings.

D. He files an unusual incident report because the person is a NYS employee who is smoking in an area where smoking is not permitted and is resisting a lawful order to stop smoking.

42. Which of the following is the next correct action for Officer Lam to take?

A. Immediately arrest the person for violating the law.

B. Remove the person from the facility, as smoking is not permitted in NYS government buildings.

C. File an unusual incident report.

D. Inform the person that smoking is not permitted in NYS government buildings.

43. Choose the best logical order of sentences from the following four choices:

A. 3 - 5 - 2 - 1 - 4   **C. 3 - 5 - 2 - 4 - 1**

B. 2 - 5 - 3 - 4 - 1   D. 5 - 3 - 2 - 4 - 1

44. Trooper Melkowitz is assigned to do a search of a cell occupied by a suspect. Based on the above, which of the following statements is the first step that Trooper Melkowitz should carry out?

A. Pat-down the inmate before he goes out of his cell.

B. Look for contraband and immediately remove it from the cell.

C. Complete Contraband Form 100-2071.

D. Instruct the offender to come out of the cell.

45. During his search, Trooper Melkowitz discovers a bayonet inside the mattress of the suspect. According to the "Procedure for a Cell Search," what is the first action that Trooper Melkowitz should take?

A. Immediately question the suspect regarding the bayonet.

B. Ask the suspects in the adjacent cells if they know anything about the bayonet.

C. Immediately report the bayonet to his sergeant so that he may take appropriate action.

D. Place the bayonet in one area of the cell and continue the search of the cell.

46. Based on the above, which of the following statements is true?

 (Choice "A" is not correct because Charles Youngs is not in his correct Unit.)

Choice "B" is not correct because Charles Youngs is not in his correct Unit.)

Choice "C" is not correct because all the inmates, except Charles Youngs, have a correct Security code.

Choice "D" is the answer because Charles Youngs is serving 30 years and 2 months (a total of 362 months). Therefore, his correct security code Level is Level "D" and he is NOT in his correct security code Level unit.

47. Which of the above four inmates is serving the least sentence?

A. James Sumpter (262 months)

B. Victor Arbor (4 years = 48 months)

C. Charles Youngs (10 years and 2 months = 122 months)

D. David Peterson (3 years and 5 months = 41 months)

48. A felon offender sentenced to 35 years shall be assigned security code level "C."

A. True in all cases.

B. False.

A felon offender sentenced to more than 360 months **(30 years)** and up to and including life in prison shall be assigned a **security code of Level D**.

C. True, only if the felony offender is over the age of 21.

D. True, if the felony offender is male.

PRACTICE TEST ANSWER KEY

1. C	13. D	25. D	37. C
2. B	14. D	26. A	38. B
3. D	15. C	27. D	39. A
4. B	16. C	28. C	40. C
5. C	17. C	29. D	41. D
6. D	18. C	30. D	42. D
7. C	19. D	31. B	43. C
8. C	20. B	32. C	44. D
9. B	21. D	33. D	45. D
10. D	22. C	34. D	46. D
11. B	23. C	35. C	47. D
12. D	24.D	36. C	48. B

Pay careful attention to every question that you don't answer correctly. If necessary, review the section in the book that relates to that type of question.

_____

12. VOCABULARY AND SPELLING WORDS

The following are important vocabulary and spelling words for police officers. Understanding the spelling and meaning of these words is helpful in answering "Understanding legal definitions," passages, "Written Expression," and "Written Comprehension" questions covered in other sections of this book. Try to study this list during brief study sessions (as opposed to a few long study sessions.) There is a theory of learning which states that students remember most when they study for short periods instead of one long period. Therefore, seven study periods during the week are more effective than one long period during the weekend.

- abide
- absence
- acceptable
- accessory
- accident
- accidentally
- accommodate
- accomplice
- achieve
- acknowledge
- acquaintance
- acquainted
- acquire
- acquit
- address
- adjacent
- admonish
- adultery
- adversary
- advisable
- affect
- affidavit
- aggravated
- aggression
- aggressive
- alias
- alibi
- allegation
- alleged
- allegiance
- amateur
- ambulance
- analysis
- angle
- annotate

- annually
- apparent
- apparently
- apprised
- approach
- arctic
- argument
- arraign
- arrest
- arson
- asphalt
- atheist
- assassination
- assailant
- August
- autopsy
- awful
- battery
- because
- becoming
- beginning
- believe
- belligerent
- bellwether
- benevolent
- bicycle
- boisterous
- burglary
- business
- calendar
- caliber
- camouflage
- capitol
- Caribbean
- category

- Caucasian
- caught
- cemetery
- changeable
- chief
- coerce
- colleague
- collectible
- collision
- column
- coming
- commit
- committed
- concealed
- concede
- congratulate
- conscientious
- conscious
- consensus
- consideration
- contempt
- continuing
- controlling
- controversy
- contusion
- conviction
- coolly
- coroner
- corroborate
- countenance
- counterfeit
- credulity
- culprit
- cumbersome
- curfew

- deceive
- defamation
- definitely
- delinquent
- derision
- desist
- desperate
- detain
- deterrent
- difference
- dilapidated
- dilemma
- disappear
- disappoint
- disastrous
- discernable
- disheveled
- disorderly
- disperse
- disturbance
- drown
- drunkenness
- dumbbell
- embarrass
- embezzlement
- emulate
- enamored
- enigma
- epilepsy
- equipment
- erratic
- exceed
- exhaust
- exhibit
- exhilarate

- existence
- exonerate
- experience
- extort
- extradition
- extreme
- famished
- farthest
- fascinating
- February
- felonious
- fictitious
- fiery
- flippant
- fluorescent
- fondle
- forcible
- foreign
- forgery
- formidable
- friend
- fugitive
- fulfil
- gauge
- government
- grateful
- guarantee
- guidance
- handicapped
- harass
- harassed
- height
- heroin
- hierarchy
- hindrance

- homicide
- humorous
- hygiene
- hypodermic
- hysterical
- ignorance
- illicit
- illiterate
- imaginary
- imbued
- imitate
- immediately
- impetuous
- incessant
- incidentally
- incoherent
- incriminating
- incursion
- independent
- indictment
- indispensable
- informant
- inhabited
- innocence
- inoculate
- insidious
- intelligence
- interfering
- interrogation
- intruder
- irrational
- jewelry
- judgment
- jurisdiction
- kernel
- laboratory
- laceration
- leisure
- lethal
- lethargic
- liaison
- library

- license
- lightning
- lose
- maintain
- maintenance
- malicious
- manslaughter
- memento
- militant
- millennium
- miniature
- minuscule
- miscellaneous
- mischief
- mischievous
- misdemeanor
- misspell
- necessary
- negligent
- neighbor
- niece
- noticeable
- notify
- obscene
- obstruct
- obvious
- occasion
- occasionally
- occult
- occurred
- occurrence
- offender
- omission
- opinion
- opium
- original
- outrageous
- pallid
- pamphlet
- paralyze
- parliament
- pastime

- perceive
- perjury
- perpetrator
- perseverance
- persistent
- personnel
- plagiarize
- playwright
- plead
- possession
- potatoes
- precede
- precedent
- prescription
- presence
- prevalent
- principle
- privilege
- probable cause
- prodigious
- professor
- prolific
- promise
- pronunciation
- proof
- prosecute
- protruding
- publicly
- puncture
- pursuit
- quarantine
- quarrel
- questionnaire
- readable
- really
- receipt
- receive
- recollection
- recommend
- reconciliation
- recurrence
- refer

- reference
- referred
- refrigerator
- registration
- regress
- relevant
- religious
- rendezvous
- repetition
- repudiate
- respiration
- restaurant
- restitution
- resuscitation
- rhyme
- rhythm
- ridiculous
- scarcely
- schedule
- secretary
- seize
- seizure
- separate
- sergeant
- siege
- significance
- silhouette
- similar
- simultaneous
- sparse
- specimen
- speech
- straighten
- strength
- subpoena
- subsidiary
- successful
- suicide
- summons
- superstitious
- suppress
- surprise

- surprised
- surveillance
- suspicious
- swerve
- syringe
- tattoo
- testify
- tetanus
- thieve
- thirtieth
- thorough
- Thursday
- tomatoes
- tomorrow
- transient
- traumatic
- Tuesday
- turbulent
- turmoil
- twelfth
- tyranny
- unconscious
- underrate
- unequivocal
- unforeseen
- until
- upholstery
- vacuum
- vandalize
- vehicle
- vehicular
- vicinity
- vicious
- visible
- warrant
- weather
- Wednesday
- weird
- welfare
- whether
- withhold

Made in the USA
Columbia, SC
26 July 2017